CRAZY EIGHTS

Fun with 8-Pointed Stars

CRAZY EIGHTS

Fun with 8-Pointed Stars

MARY SUE SUIT

Martingale®
& COMPANY

Credits

President · *Nancy J. Martin*
CEO · *Daniel J. Martin*
VP and General Manager · *Tom Wierzbicki*
Publisher · *Jane Hamada*
Editorial Director · *Mary V. Green*
Managing Editor · *Tina Cook*
Technical Editor · *Laurie Baker*
Copy Editor · *Durby Peterson*
Design Director · *Stan Green*
Illustrator · *Laurel Strand*
Cover and Text Designer · *Trina Craig*
Photographer · *Brent Kane*

That Patchwork Place® is an imprint
of Martingale & Company®.

Crazy Eights: Fun with 8-Pointed Stars
© 2005 by Mary Sue Suit

Martingale & Company
20205 144th Avenue NE
Woodinville, WA 98072-8478 USA
www.martingale-pub.com

Printed in China
10 09 08 07 06 05   8 7 6 5 4 3 2 1

Library of Congress Cataloging-in-Publication Data
Suit, Mary Sue.
   Crazy eights : fun with 8-pointed stars / Mary Sue Suit.
      p. cm.
   ISBN 1-56477-601-8
   1. Patchwork—Patterns. 2. Quilting. 3. Star quilts. I. Title.
   TT835.S8224 2005
   746.46'041—dc22   2005003481

Mission Statement
Dedicated to providing quality
products and service to inspire creativity.

Dedication

To Judy—you know why.

Acknowledgments

Many thanks to:

- The ladies of Chadron Quilt Guild for their encouragement

- The participants at Black Hills Quilt Retreat for always wanting something new and being brave enough to try it

- Mary Ellen Reynolds, Becky Umenthum, and Dorothy Wittig for their quilts

- Melissa Johnson and Woody Woodworth for their "Quilt Ferry" service

- Hobbs Bonded Fibers. Your wool batting is great!

Contents

Introduction

*T*HE QUILTS IN this book are all created with Eight-Pointed Star blocks. But these are no ordinary eight-pointed stars. They are made by joining large, pieced 45° triangles together. It sounds hard and they look intricate, but once you master a few cutting and trimming techniques for building the stars from a basic pieced triangle unit, you'll discover all kinds of ways to take your stars from ordinary to stellar.

Twelve Eight-Pointed Star block variations are used throughout the book. Each block finishes to 16" x 16" so you can substitute any of the blocks in any of the quilt designs. You'll learn how to piece each variation in "Crazy Eights Sampler" on page 25 and then assemble them into a quilt. You don't have to start with this project, but it does give you a good view of all the different ways the stars can be created. The blocks are presented in order from easiest to most complex, so I suggest beginning with the Basic Star: Blocks 1 and 2. Consider using any of the Star blocks on their own as well. With the addition of a couple of borders, they make a lovely small wall hanging like the one you see at left.

Along with the Star block variations, you will also learn to make the single and double Lunatic Fringe blocks. These blocks are so easy it's crazy. Like the Star blocks, they begin with a pieced triangle unit, so any pieced triangle unit you use in a Star block can be substituted in the Lunatic Fringe blocks. Use the blocks on their own or in combination with the Star blocks to open up a whole new dimension of possibilities.

But that's not all. The border treatments are out of this world as well. Like the blocks, they are much simpler to create than they appear. For many, you will use a pair of triangle units in the corners. The treatment gives the quilt a nice rounded appearance and eliminates the need to miter the corners.

Before you embark on your journey into the stars, please read through the basic instructions for cutting each element used to make the blocks, presented in "Cutting the Pieces" on page 13, and the specifics for making the pieced triangle unit and the Lunatic Fringe blocks, given on page 16. I also recommend the warm-up project on page 21, "Just Triangles," to get you acquainted with working with the triangular shapes. From there, the sampler quilt will familiarize you with the star piecing technique, and then the sky is the limit!

OPPOSITE: MARY'S STAR. Pieced and quilted by Dorothy Wittig.
Finished block size: 22" x 22"
Dorothy participated in my first experimental Crazy Eights class. She chose to make this practice star as a small wall hanging or tabletop piece.

General Information

*T*HIS CHAPTER COVERS what you'll need to make your quilts a shining success.

BASIC SUPPLIES

You will need scissors, a sewing machine, a rotary cutter and mat, and an 8½" x 24" quilter's ruler for cutting strips of fabric and squaring up pieces.

MARY SUE'S TRIANGLE RULER®

You can use a handmade template to make the pieced triangle units and Lunatic Fringe blocks in this book (the necessary template pattern is included on page 93), but you might want to consider replacing the template with Mary Sue's Triangle Ruler, a tool specially designed for making pieced triangle units. Mary Sue's Triangle Ruler is a quadrangle with 45°, 90°, and 112.5° corners.

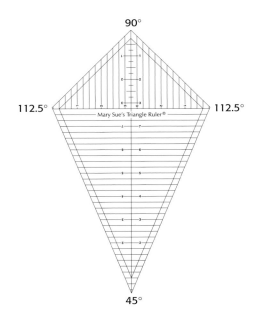

Two important lines divide the ruler into sections: the centerline runs from the 45° corner to the 90° corner, and the crossbar connects the two 112.5° angles. In addition, ¼" seam-allowance lines run parallel to the edges of the ruler.

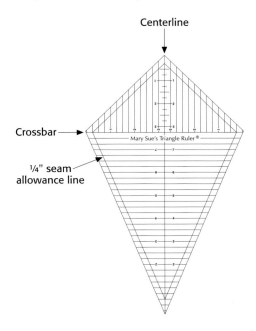

To cut the 45° triangles used for the quilts in this book, place the ruler as shown, so that the crossbar is horizontal. The crossbar marks the short side of the triangle. The lines that run parallel to the crossbar indicate the size of the piece.

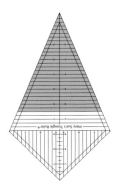

FABRIC SELECTION

Your choice of fabrics is what determines how brightly your stars will shine. Contrast is the key to seeing all the points. Think about the sky. The stars are always present, but they can only be seen against the dark contrast of the night sky. It is important to make sure your star points will be seen.

Do not place star points made of medium-value fabrics on a medium-value background if you really want to make your quilt sparkle. This is especially important when using a background fabric with a large-scale print, such as the one I used in "Crazy Eights Sampler" on page 25. You can see that there are a few blocks where the points are lost in the print. Using a darker fabric for the star points would have made them clearly visible.

If you remember that contrast in value (the darkness or lightness of the fabric) is what you are looking for, your stars will stand out. Try making a

black-and-white copy of the fabrics to help you assign the color values within the quilt.

The important question to keep asking yourself is, "Will I see the points?"

PRESSING

Make sure you press, press, and press. It is one of the most important steps to a great quilt top, no matter what pattern you use. The object of pressing is not to make the fabric warm but to make the seams lie flat. If your piecing does not lie flat after pressing, get back up and press it again. I keep my ironing board and sewing machine at different ends of the room to add a little exercise to my day.

I think I stumbled onto the answer to the steam-or-not-to-steam question. As usual, it depends. I live in a semiarid climate and have always used steam because it produces the desired result (and provides a beauty-treatment opportunity). However, after working in a very humid Maine environment for several weeks, it became apparent that a dry iron was the way to go. If you are wondering what will work best for you, check the humidity in your environment and set the iron accordingly.

You can press your seams in any direction that works best for you. I have found that it often varies from block to block, as well as from setting to setting. The pressing suggestions that follow are based on my experience.

I love to hand quilt, so I usually press the seams toward the darker fabric or to the side that will create the least bulk. I am also not shy about trimming out bulky intersections. If you machine quilt, press the seams in the direction that will be easiest for you to handle. If you send your tops out to be machine quilted, consult your quilter. She is a very important person in your life. I have found that when it comes to quilting, you never want to upset your machine quilter or your mechanic.

Cutting the Pieces

 *F*OR THE QUILTS in this book, all the pieces are cut from strips. The fabric requirements are based on a usable width of 40", but your fabric may be slightly wider, so cut one strip at a time, cut the required pieces from it, and then cut another strip if needed. You may need fewer strips than what is called for.

All the quilts in this book were made using Mary Sue's Triangle Ruler, described on page 11. They can also be made using the template pattern on page 93. The template is not a duplicate of the ruler but provides the shape and measurements needed to cut the pieces. The projects employ several cutting and trimming methods to cut the different pieces. Remember that you can substitute two cuts from a fat quarter for a full-width strip if necessary.

NOTE: *The ruler is shown in the illustrations throughout the book.*

BACKGROUND TRIANGLES

Used in the basic pieced triangle units, these are cut from strips that always measure 5¼" wide. You will be able to cut eight pairs of triangles (16 total) from each folded 5¼" x 42" strip.

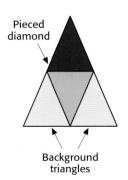

Pieced diamond

Background triangles

To cut the background triangles:

1. Fold the 5¼" x 42" strip in half crosswise. Place the triangle ruler or template on the strip just inside the selvages, with the 5¼" line aligned with the bottom edge of the strip. Cut along both ruler or template edges.

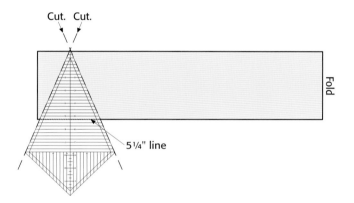

Cut. Cut.

5¼" line

Fold

2. Rotate the ruler or template so that the 5¼" line is aligned with the top edge of the strip and the side of the ruler or template is aligned with the previous cut. Then cut along the right edge of the ruler or template.

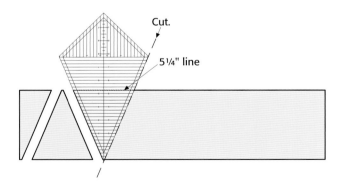

Cut.

5¼" line

3. Continue rotating the ruler or template in this manner to cut triangles from the remainder of the strip.

    NOTE: *You need two background triangles for each pieced triangle unit, so leave your fabric strip folded while cutting. Keep the triangles in pairs to help your piecing session go smoothly.*

LARGE 45° TRIANGLES

These triangles are the same size as the basic pieced triangle unit. They are cut the same as the background triangles but from a 9"-wide strip. Mary Sue's Triangle Ruler is not quite large enough to cut across the 9" strip, so some sliding is necessary.

1. Fold the 9" x 42" strip in half crosswise. Place the ruler or template on the strip with the 45° tip facing downward and the centerline on the selvages. Align the 2" line on the 90° corner of the ruler with the top edge of the strip. Beginning at the bottom of the ruler, cut along the right side of the ruler as far as you can, and then slide the ruler up to make the full cut, keeping the edge of the ruler aligned with the edge you just cut. Discard the piece cut from the end of the strip or set it aside for use in another project.

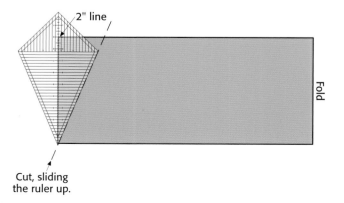

2" line

Fold

Cut, sliding the ruler up.

2. Rotate the ruler or template so that the 2" line on the 90° corner of the ruler is aligned with the bottom edge of the strip. Cut along the right edge of the ruler, beginning the cut halfway down the ruler and cutting up. Slide the ruler down to finish the cut in the same manner as before.

Cut, starting halfway down the ruler and cutting up and then sliding the ruler down to complete the cut.

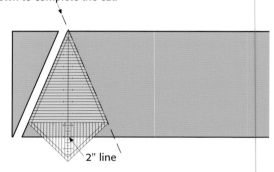

2" line

3. Continue in this manner to cut triangles from the remainder of the strip.

90° TRIANGLES

NOTE: *For simplicity, I refer to these shapes as 90° triangles throughout the book, although they are actually four-sided when cut and do not become three-sided until sewn.*

These triangles are used on the sides of 45° triangles to give you a straight edge to work with. There are two methods for cutting the triangles, depending on what other pieces you need from the same fabric. They are cut in pairs from either a folded strip of fabric or from two rectangles that have been layered with the same sides together. This ensures that you have a right and a left piece.

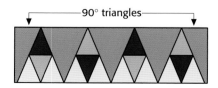

90° triangles

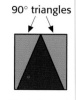

90° triangles

Single Lunatic Fringe block

Method 1

Use this method when you need to cut 90° triangles plus large 45° triangles from the same fabric.

1. Cut a strip 9" x 42".

2. Fold the strip in half crosswise and remove the selvages.

3. At the top of the strip, measure 4¼" from the left edge and make a mark.

4. Place the ruler or template on the strip with the tip at the 4¼" mark and the 2" line on the 90° corner of the ruler aligned with the bottom edge of the strip as shown. Beginning at the tip, cut along both edges of the ruler, sliding the ruler down as described in "Large 45° Triangles" at left to make the full cut. This will yield one set of 90° triangles plus two large 45° triangles. You can then continue cutting triangles as described previously until you have the necessary amount.

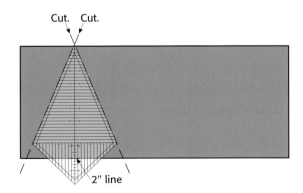

If you need more than one set of 90° triangles, align the 4¼" line of your straight-edge rotary ruler where the tip of the last triangle was

cut. Cut along the right edge of the ruler to yield one additional set.

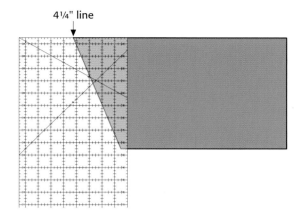

Method 2

Use this method when you need only 90° triangles. Each pair of rectangles will yield two sets of 90° triangles.

1. Cut two 4½" x 9" rectangles from the required fabric.

2. Layer the rectangles right sides together as shown. At the top of the rectangles, measure 4¼" from the left edge and make a mark. At the bottom of the rectangles, measure ¼" from the left edge and make a mark.

3. Place a straight-edged rotary ruler on the rectangles to connect the marks; cut to yield two sets.

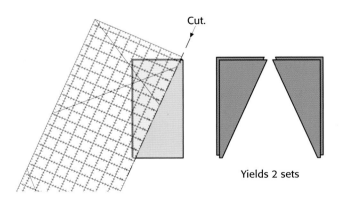

Yields 2 sets

Assembling the Pieced Triangle Unit and Lunatic Fringe Blocks

THE QUILTS IN this book are made using one or more of the three elements presented in this chapter: the basic pieced triangle unit, the Single Lunatic Fringe block, and the Double Lunatic Fringe block.

BASIC PIECED TRIANGLE UNIT

The basic pieced triangle unit consists of a pieced diamond and one pair of background triangles. Several variations of the pieced diamond are used throughout the book, but the basic construction of the triangle unit is the same.

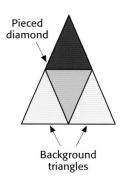

Pieced diamond

Background triangles

1. Layer the two 5¼"-wide strips indicated in the project instructions right sides together. Sew ¼" from the top and bottom edges.

2. Place the triangle ruler or template on the strip with the 4¾" line aligned with the seam at the bottom of the strip. The tip of the ruler or template will be at the seam line across the top of the strip. Cut along both sides of the ruler to cut one pieced diamond.

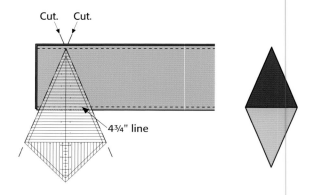

Cut. Cut.

4¾" line

3. Rotate the ruler or template so that the 4¾" line is aligned with the seam line at the top of the strip. Cut along the right side of the ruler. Continue rotating the ruler in this manner to cut the required number of pieces. Press the seams open to reveal the pieced diamonds. You should be able to cut 8 pieced diamonds from a 5¼" x 21" strip or 16 pieced diamonds from a 5¼" x 42" strip.

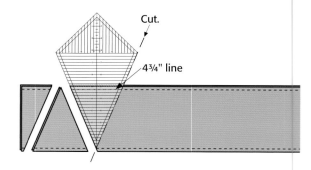

Cut.

4¾" line

4. Position a background triangle on the upper-right edge of each pieced diamond, right sides together as shown. Match the top corner of the triangle to the tip of the diamond. The tip of the triangle will extend below the seam of the pieced diamond. Stitch ¼" from the edge. Press the seam toward the background triangle.

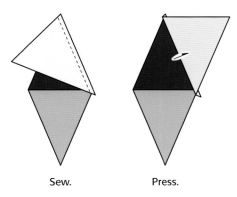

Sew.   Press.

5. Repeat to add the background triangle to the upper-left edge of each pieced diamond. Press the seam toward the diamond.

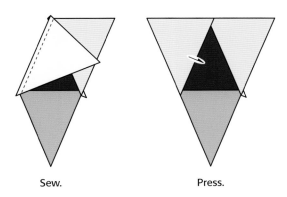

Sew.   Press.

Tip

It is easier to match the points on complex blocks if you stitch with the pieced unit on top.

6. Trim the pieced triangle units. Place a pieced triangle unit on the cutting surface with the background triangles at the bottom as shown. Position the triangle ruler or template on the unit with the 4¾" line on the horizontal seam line of the pieced diamond and the 2¼" line on the 90° corner of the ruler at the lower tip of the pieced diamond as shown. The ¼" side seam line on the ruler should cross the seam intersections of the pieced diamond and background triangles. Trim any excess. You will need to slide the ruler down along the trimmed upper side edges to trim the lower side edges.

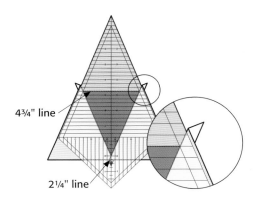

4¾" line

2¼" line

NOTE: *These measurements depend on a full ¼" seam allowance. If your triangle is a bit large, check your seams and adjust as necessary.*

7. Turn the pieced triangle unit so the background triangles are at the top as shown. Position the triangle ruler on the unit with the crossbar line on the trimmed left side edge and the ¼" seam allowance aligned across the tip of the pieced diamond. Cut across the background triangles to complete the trimming process.

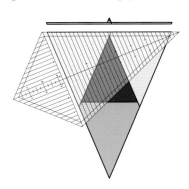

SINGLE LUNATIC FRINGE BLOCK

This block is made up of a large 45° triangle and a right-side and left-side 90° triangle. The 45° triangle can be plain or pieced.

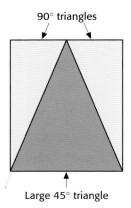

90° triangles

Large 45° triangle

1. With right sides together, sew a right-side 90° triangle to the right edge of a large 45° triangle or pieced triangle unit. Press the seam toward the 90° triangle.

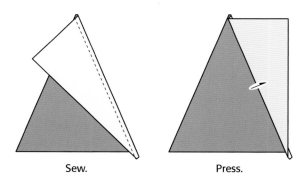

Sew.   Press.

2. Repeat step 1 to sew the left-side 90° triangle to the left edge of the large 45° triangle or pieced triangle unit.

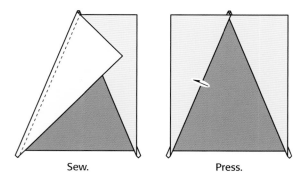

Sew.   Press.

3. Trim the block to 7" x 8½". To trim the block evenly, place the block on the cutting surface with the triangle point at the bottom as shown. Using a ruler that is at least 8½" wide, position the 8¼" horizontal line at the triangle tip, the 3½" vertical line through the center of the triangle, and the 7" vertical line on the left edge. Trim along the right edge and top of the block. The narrow end of the 90° triangle on the right side should measure ¼" from the triangle point to the block edge.

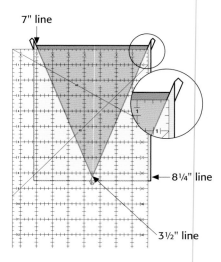

7" line

8¼" line

3½" line

4. Rotate the block so the triangle point is at the top as shown. Position the ruler on the block with the 8½" horizontal line at the bottom of the block, the 7" vertical line on the left edge, and the 3½" vertical line through the center of the triangle. Trim along the right edge and top of the block.

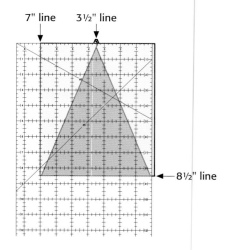

7" line   3½" line

8½" line

DOUBLE LUNATIC FRINGE BLOCK

This block looks like two Single Lunatic Fringe blocks stacked on top of each other with the points meeting in the middle, except that there is no center seam. You will begin by cutting two 8" x 18" rectangles, one each of two different fabrics, in half twice diagonally. Each rectangle will yield two large 45° triangles and two side triangles. A pieced triangle can be substituted for the large 45° triangle. In the projects in this book where that has been done, the plain 45° triangles are used elsewhere in the project so as not to waste them.

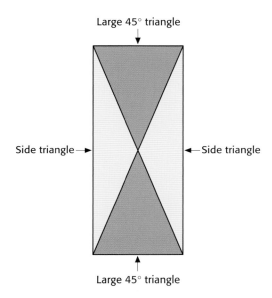

Large 45° triangle

Side triangle →   ← Side triangle

Large 45° triangle

1. On each end of *each* 8" x 18" rectangle, measure ¼" in from both long edges and make a mark. Using your rotary cutter and a long ruler, connect the marks diagonally and cut each rectangle in half. Without moving the pieces, cut each rectangle across the opposite diagonal.

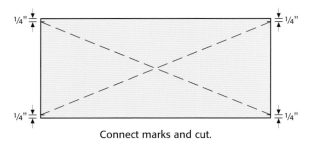

Connect marks and cut.

2. With right sides together, place a side triangle from one rectangle on the right edge of each of the two 45° triangles from the other rectangle. Extend the point of the 45° triangle above the point of the side triangle so that the first stitch will go through both pieces of fabric; stitch. Press the seams in the same direction.

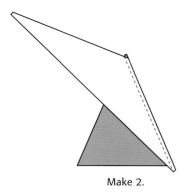

Make 2.

3. Sew the two halves together. The seams should cross at the ¼" mark so the tips of the large triangles will match and be sharp.

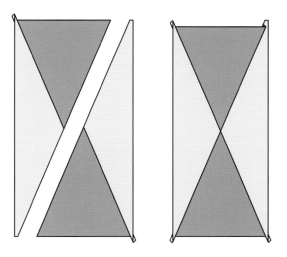

4. Trim the block to 7" x 16½". To trim the block evenly, lay it horizontally on the cutting surface. Place a long rotary cutting ruler on the block with the 8¼" vertical line positioned where the tips of the 45° triangles meet and the ¼" horizontal line positioned at the base point of the 45° triangle as shown. Trim along the right edge and top of the block.

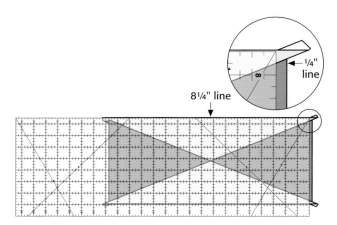

Tip

When setting up your cutting space, place your mat on a corner of your table. I am right-handed, so I place my mat on the left-hand corner closest to me. This position allows me to easily make horizontal cuts and step around the corner to make vertical cuts without moving the fabric.

5. Rotate the block 180°. Align the left edge of the block with the 16½" vertical line on the ruler, the tips of the 45° triangles with the 8¼" vertical line, and the base point of the 45° triangle with the ¼" horizontal line as shown. Trim along the right edge and top of the block.

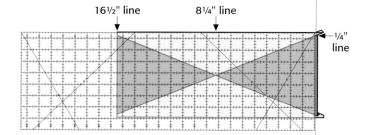

Just Triangles

Pieced and quilted by Mary Ellen Reynolds

*T*HIS PROJECT WILL give you practice making the basic pieced triangle and help you develop a feel for value placement. Without taking a lot of time, it offers a good opportunity to use up some of your smaller pieces and fabrics that fall into the "I wonder why I purchased it" pile (which we all have). The finished quilt is large enough for many children's community service projects, but once you get started, you may not want to stop. If that is the case, simply continue to make triangles until the quilt is as large as you want. When you run out of a fabric, find one of similar color and value and keep going for a scrappy appearance. A diagram for a 74" x 80" quilt is given on page 24.

Finished quilt size: 34" x 40"

MATERIALS

Yardages are based on 42"-wide fabrics.
- ¾ yard of maroon print for pieced triangle units and border
- ½ yard of dark green print for pieced triangle units, 90° triangles, and binding
- ½ yard of medium green print for pieced triangle units and large 45° triangles
- ½ yard of light mauve print for pieced triangle units, large 45° triangles, and 90° triangles
- ¼ yard of light green print for pieced triangle units
- ¼ yard of medium mauve print for pieced triangle units, large 45° triangles, and 90° triangles
- 1½ yards of fabric for backing
- ¾ yard of fabric for binding
- 40" x 44" piece of batting

CUTTING

All measurements include ¼-wide seam allowances. Refer to "Cutting the Pieces" on page 13 for specifics on cutting the background triangles, large 45° triangles, and 90° triangles.

From the medium mauve print, cut:
- 1 strip, 9" x 21"; cut 1 set of 90° triangles and 3 large 45° triangles
- 1 strip, 5¼" x 21"

From the maroon print, cut:
- 1 strip, 5¼" x 21"
- 2 strips, 4½" x 32½"
- 2 strips, 4½" x 34½"

From the light mauve print, cut:
- 1 strip, 5¼" x 42"; cut 8 pairs of background triangles (16 total)
- 1 strip, 9" x 21"; cut 1 set of 90° triangles and 3 large 45° triangles

From the medium green print, cut:
- 1 strip, 9" x 42"; cut 2 sets of 90° triangles and 6 large 45° triangles
- 1 strip, 5¼" x 21"

From the dark green print, cut:
- 1 strip, 5¼" x 21"

From the light green print, cut:
- 1 strip, 5¼" x 42"; cut 8 pairs of background triangles (16 total)

MAKING THE PIECED TRIANGLE UNITS

1. Refer to "Basic Pieced Triangle Unit" on page 16 to layer the medium mauve and maroon 5¼" x 21" strips and cut eight pieced diamonds. Stitch the light mauve background triangles to the pieced diamonds as shown. Make four of each coloration.

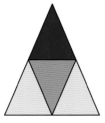
Make 4.

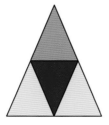
Make 4.

2. Repeat step 1 with the medium green and dark green 5¼" x 21" strips and the light green background triangles to make the green pieced triangle units as shown.

Make 4.

Make 4.

ASSEMBLING THE QUILT TOP

1. Lay out the pieced triangle units, large 45° triangles, and 90° triangles into four horizontal rows as shown, or create your own strip pattern. Stitch the pieces in each row together. Use a ruler to make sure the rows are 8½" wide and that the points of the 45° triangles are at the 2¾" line on the 90° corner of the ruler. There should be 6½" between the tips of the pieced diamonds. The first and last seams of each row should be ¼" from the end of the row.

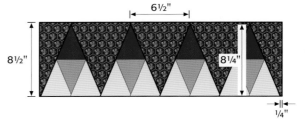

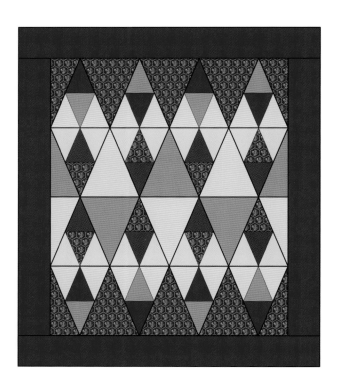

2. Sew the rows together.

3. Sew the 4½" x 32½" maroon strips to the sides of the quilt top. Press the seams toward the border strips. Sew the 4½" x 34½" maroon strips to the top and bottom edges of the quilt top. Press the seams toward the border strips.

FINISHING THE QUILT

Refer to "Techniques for Finishing" on page 89.

1. Layer the quilt top with batting and backing; baste.

2. Hand or machine quilt as desired.

3. Bind the quilt edges.

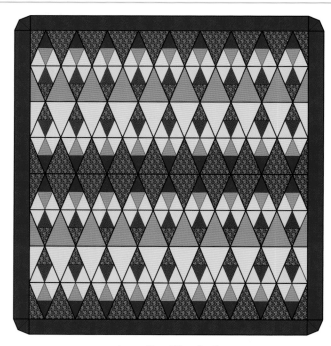

Large "Just Triangles,"
approximately 74" x 80"

JUST TRIANGLES VARIATION

To make a larger, 74" x 80" version of "Just Triangles," stitch together longer rows. For *each* row, you will need:

- 2 strips, 5¼" x 21", for pieced diamonds
- 2 strips, 5¼" x 21", for background triangles
- 2 strips, 9" x 21", for large 45° triangles

Cut the borders 8½" wide and add two large 45° triangles in each corner.

CRAZY EIGHTS SAMPLER

Pieced and quilted by Mary Sue Suit

*T*HIS QUILT IS made up of the twelve Eight-Pointed Star block variations you will use throughout the projects in this book. Each star is made up of eight pieced triangle units, but the pieced diamond in each unit is different for each block. For this project, you can choose to make each of the different blocks or just pick the one you like best and make all the blocks the same. The border treatment will work with all of them.

Finished quilt size: 78" x 94" · Finished Star block size: 16" x 16" · Finished Corner Star block size: 8" x 8"

MATERIALS

Yardages are based on 42"-wide fabrics.

- ½ yard *each* of 12 assorted blue fabrics for block stars and inner pieced-border corner stars
- 3¼ yards of blue-and-yellow fabric for block backgrounds, inner pieced border, and middle border
- 3 yards of white fabric for block corners, inner pieced border, and middle-border corner squares
- 1⅝ yards of dark blue fabric for outer border
- 5½ yards of fabric for backing
- 1 yard of fabric for binding
- 82" x 98" piece of batting

CUTTING

All measurements include ¼"-wide seam allowances. Refer to "Cutting the Pieces" on page 13 for specifics on cutting the background triangles and large 45° triangles.

All Blocks and Borders

From the blue-and-yellow fabric, cut:

- 12 strips, 5¼" x 42"; cut 96 sets of background triangles (192 total)
- 2 strips, 9" x 42"; cut 14 large 45° triangles
- 8 inner-border strips, 2½" x 42"

From the white fabric, cut:

- 6 strips, 8½" x 42"
- 4 strips, 6" x 42"; crosscut into 24 squares, 6" x 6". Cut each square in half once diagonally to yield 48 triangles.
- 1 strip, 3¼" x 42"; crosscut into 8 squares, 3¼" x 3¼". Cut each square in half once diagonally to yield 16 triangles.
- 4 squares, 2½" x 2½"

From the dark blue fabric for outer border, cut:

- 9 strips, 5½" x 42"

Block 1
From *each* of 2 assorted blue fabrics, cut:

- 1 strip, 5¼" x 21"

Block 2
From *each* of 2 assorted blue fabrics, cut:

- 1 strip, 5¼" x 21"

Block 3
From *each* of 2 assorted blue fabrics, cut:

- 1 strip, 5¼" x 21"

Block 4
From *each* of 4 assorted blue fabrics (select 4 that range from light to dark), cut:

- 1 strip, 2⅞" x 21"

Block 5
From *each* of 4 assorted blue fabrics (select 4 that range from light to dark), cut:

- 1 strip, 2⅞" x 21"

Blocks 6 and 7

From the blue-and-yellow fabric, cut:
- 1 strip, 2¾" x 42"

From *each* of 2 assorted blue fabrics, cut:
- 2 strips, 5" x 21"

Block 8

From *each* of 2 assorted blue fabrics, cut:
- 2 strips, 2¾" x 21"

From a different assorted blue fabric, cut:
- 2 strips, 3½" x 21"

Block 9

From *each* of 2 assorted blue fabrics, cut:
- 2 strips, 2¾" x 21"
- 1 strip, 3½" x 21"

Blocks 10 and 11

From 1 assorted blue fabric, cut:
- 5 strips, 3½" x 21" (A)

From a different assorted blue fabric, cut:
- 4 strips, 3½" x 21" (B)

From another assorted blue fabric, cut:
- 1 strip, 3½" x 15½" (C) (for block 10 only)
- 2 strips, 3¼" x 15½" (C) (for block 10 only)
- 2 strips, 3" x 27½" (C) (for block 11 only)

Block 12

From 1 assorted blue fabric, cut:
- 1 strip, 3" x 21"
- 1 rectangle, 3" x 5¼"

From a different assorted blue fabric, cut:
- 1 strip, 3" x 21"

From another assorted blue fabric, cut:
- 1 strip, 5¼" x 27½"

Corner Star Blocks

From the white fabric, cut:
- 3 strips, 3¼" x 42"

From *each* of 2 assorted blue fabrics, cut:
- 1 strip, 3¼" x 42"
- 1 rectangle, 3¼" x 8"

BASIC STAR: BLOCKS 1 AND 2

1. *To make block 1,* refer to "Basic Pieced Triangle Unit" on page 16 to layer the 5¼" x 21" strips together; stitch along both long edges. From the layered and stitched strips, cut eight pieced diamonds.

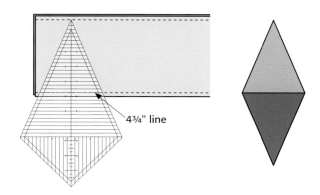

4¾" line

2. Sew two background triangles to the same color in each pieced diamond to make the pieced triangle units as shown.

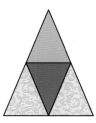

Make 8.

3. Stitch two pieced triangle units together as shown. Make four pairs. Press the seams in one direction and then trim the dog-ears.

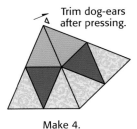

Trim dog-ears after pressing.

Make 4.

TIP

Make sure your seams match each time you join pieces. If the seams do not match each time, every additional piece added will make the problem worse.

4. Sew two pairs of units together to make one octagon half as shown. Make two halves. Press the seams in the same direction as before.

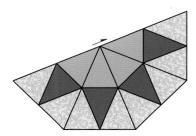

Make 2.

5. Sew the two halves together.

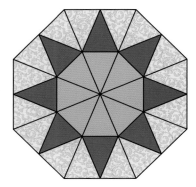

Make 1.

NOTE: *For all of the Star blocks, trim any threads that extend above the center seam. Hold the center seam close to each side of the vertical seam that intersects it. Give the center seam a twist. That should undo the stitches above the center seam, allowing you to press the seam in one direction around the octagon.*

6. Fold four white 6" corner triangles in half, wrong side together, to find the center of the long edge. With right sides together, place a triangle on each diagonal edge of the octagon as shown. Match the center point of the long edge with the tip of the star; stitch. Press the seams toward the corner triangles.

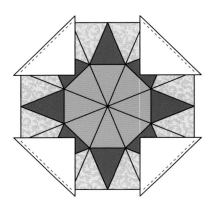

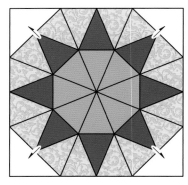

Block 1

7. Trim the block to 16½" x 16½". To trim the block evenly, place a ruler that is at least 16½" square on the block with the 8¼" marks at the tip of the top diamond and the right side diamond. Trim any excess along the top and right side edges. Rotate the block 180° and repeat to trim the remaining two sides. You may also use an 8½" square ruler and trim each corner separately.

8. *To make block 2,* refer to "Basic Pieced Triangle Unit" on page 16 to layer the 5¼" x 21" strips together; stitch along both long edges. From the layered and stitched strips, cut eight pieced diamonds. Sew two background triangles to the same color in four pieced diamonds and to the opposite color in the remaining four pieced diamonds as shown.

Make 4.   Make 4.

9. Repeat steps 2–6 to make the block, alternating the pieced triangle units so that every other triangle has the opposite color pointing toward the center.

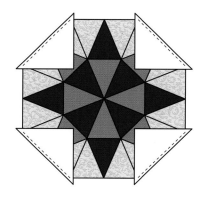

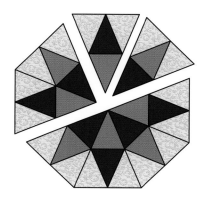

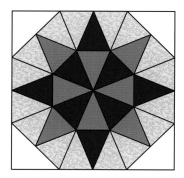

Block 2

SQUASHED BASIC STAR: BLOCK 3

1. Refer to "Basic Pieced Triangle Unit" on page 16 to layer the 5¼" x 21" strips together; stitch along both long edges. "Squash" the tube so that the seams match in the center of the tube. Press the tube lightly. Cut the pieced diamonds as you normally would, but align the 4¾" line of the triangle ruler with the fold lines instead of the seam lines. Cut eight pieced diamonds. You will have four of each of the two colorations.

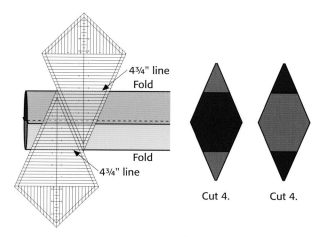

4¾" line
Fold

Fold
4¾" line

Cut 4.   Cut 4.

2. Sew two background triangles to each pieced diamond as shown.

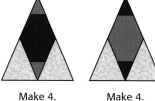

Make 4.   Make 4.

3. Refer to steps 2–7 of "Basic Star: Blocks 1 and 2" on pages 27 and 28 to sew the triangle units together as shown, add the corner triangles, and trim the block.

Block 3

FOUR-COLOR STAR: BLOCK 4

1. Arrange the 2⅞" x 21" strips in order from light to dark and label them A–D in that order.

2. Sew strips A and B together along the long edges. Repeat with strips C and D. Press the seams toward B and D.

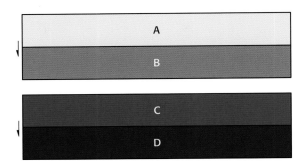

3. With right sides together, lay strip set CD on strip set AB so that the A and D strips and the B and C strips are together. Stitch ¼" from both long edges. Refer to "Basic Pieced Triangle Unit" on page 16 to cut eight pieced diamonds from the layered strips. You will have four of each of the two colorations.

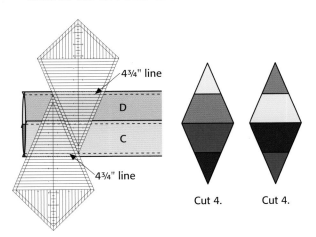

Cut 4. Cut 4.

4. Sew two background triangles to each pieced diamond as shown.

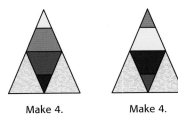

Make 4. Make 4.

5. Refer to steps 2–7 of "Basic Star: Blocks 1 and 2" on pages 27 and 28 to sew the triangle units together as shown, add the corner triangles, and trim the block.

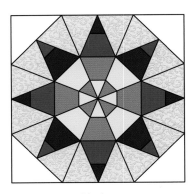

Block 4

SQUASHED FOUR-COLOR STAR: BLOCK 5

1. Arrange the 2⅞" x 21" strips in order from light to dark and label them A–D in that order.

2. Sew strips A and B together along the long edges. Repeat with strips C and D. Press the seams toward B and D.

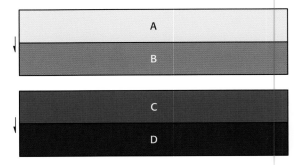

3. With right sides together, lay strip set CD on strip set AB so that the A and D strips and the B and C strips are together. Stitch ¼" from both long edges. "Squash" the tube so the B and D strips are aligned in the center of the tube as shown. Lightly press the tube. Cut the pieced diamonds as you normally would, but align the 4¾" line of the triangle ruler with the fold lines instead of the seam lines. Cut eight pieced diamonds. You will have four of each of the two colorations.

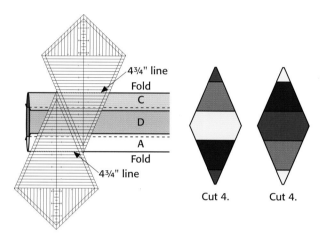

Cut 4.   Cut 4.

TIP

If the diamonds are still joined after cutting, just snip them apart at the tip.

4. Sew two background triangles to each pieced diamond as shown.

Make 4.   Make 4.

5. Refer to steps 2–7 of "Basic Star: Blocks 1 and 2" on pages 27 and 28 to sew the triangle units together as shown, add the corner triangles, and trim the block.

Block 5

SINGLE-TIPPED CHECKERBOARD STAR: BLOCK 6 AND STELLAR BUDDY STAR: BLOCK 7

1. Sew the 5" x 21" strips together along the long edges, alternating fabrics. Press the seams open.

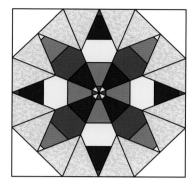

TIP

Hold the ends of one seam and give it a gentle tug. Repeat with the remaining seams. This will release the tension and allow the seams to lie straight and open easier. Make sure you are gentle. Don't break the threads.

2. Fold the strip set in half crosswise; finger-press the fold. Open up the fabric and cut along the fold line. Stitch the two halves together, side by side, making sure the colors alternate.

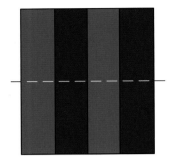

Cut in half.

Stitch halves together.

3. Turn the strip set so the strips are horizontal. Even up one long edge of the strip set, and then cut one 5¼"-wide segment and one 3"-wide segment.

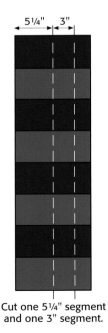

Cut one 5¼" segment
and one 3" segment.

4. Remove the first two pieces of the leftover strip-set segment. Stitch a piece to the ends of each segment from step 3 as shown, maintaining the color sequence and aligning the long edge of each piece with one of the strip-set short edges. The piece stitched to the 5¼"-wide segment will be ¼" shorter but will not affect the diamond-cutting process. Position the extra piece even with the bottom of the strip. The piece stitched to the 3"-wide segment will be wider than the strip set; cut the edge that extends beyond the strip even with the long edge.

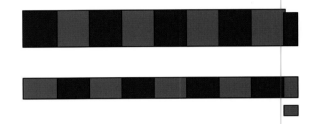

5. Sew the 2¾" x 42" background strip to the long edge of the 3"-wide strip-set segment.

6. With right sides together, lay the 5¼"-wide strip-set segment over the segment from step 5. Be sure that each strip-set segment is aligned with a different color segment and that the seams match. Stitch ¼" from both long edges.

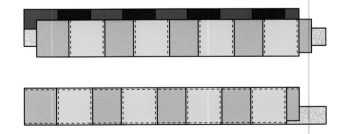

7. Lay the stitched strips on your cutting surface so that the strip from step 5 is on the bottom as shown. Refer to "Basic Pieced Triangle Unit" on page 16 to cut the pieced diamonds, placing the 4¾" line of the ruler on the seam and the ruler centerline on the strip-set seam line. Cut 16 pieced diamonds. You will have four of each of the four pieced diamonds.

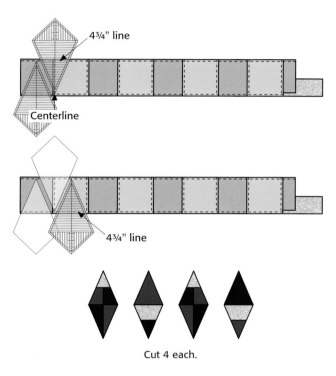

Cut 4 each.

8. Sew two background triangles to each pieced diamond as shown.

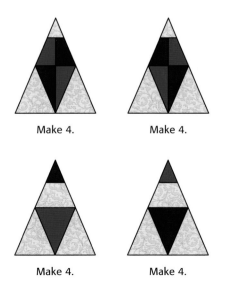

Make 4.　　Make 4.

Make 4.　　Make 4.

9. Refer to steps 2–7 of "Basic Star: Blocks 1 and 2" on pages 27 and 28 to sew the triangle units together as shown for each block, add the corner triangles, and trim the blocks.

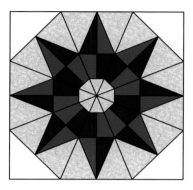

Block 6

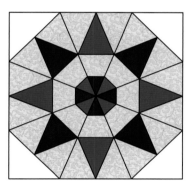

Block 7

SINGLE-COLOR DOUBLE-TIPPED CHECKERBOARD STAR: BLOCK 8

1. Sew the 2¾" x 21" strips together along the long edges, alternating fabrics. Press the seams open.

2. Fold the strip set in half crosswise; finger-press the fold. Open up the fabric and cut along the fold line. Stitch the two halves together side by side, making sure the colors alternate.

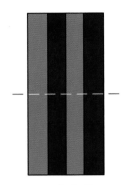

Cut in half.

Stitch halves together.

3. Turn the strip set so the strips are horizontal. Even up one long edge of the strip set, and then cut four 2¼"-wide segments.

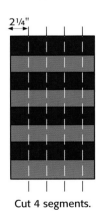

Cut 4 segments.

4. Stitch a 3½" x 21" strip to one long edge of two strip-set segments as shown, aligning the left ends. The 3½" strips will be longer than the strip-set segments. Press the seams toward the 3½"-wide strips.

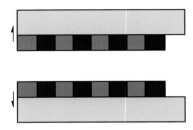

5. Stitch the remaining strip-set segments to the long edges of the 3½"-wide strips as shown, off-setting the newly attached segment with the previously attached segment so that different colors are opposite each other and the seams are aligned.

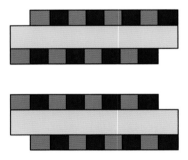

6. Lay the pieces from step 5 right sides together as shown. Stitch ¼" from the long edges.

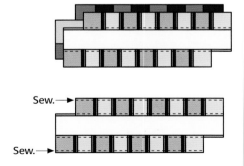

Sew. →

Sew. →

7. Refer to "Basic Pieced Triangle Unit" on page 16 to cut the pieced diamonds, placing the 4¾" line of the ruler on the seam and the ruler centerline on the strip-set seam line. Cut eight pieced diamonds. You will have four of each of the two colorations.

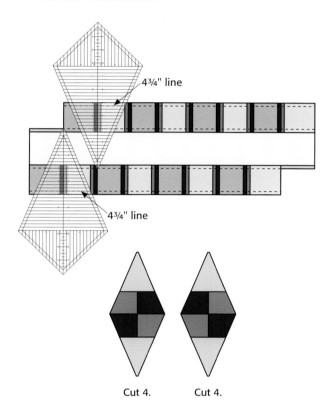

Cut 4.   Cut 4.

8. Sew two background triangles to each pieced diamond as shown.

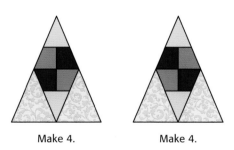

Make 4.   Make 4.

9. Refer to steps 2–7 of "Basic Star: Blocks 1 and 2" on pages 27 and 28 to sew the triangle units together as shown, add the corner triangles, and trim the block.

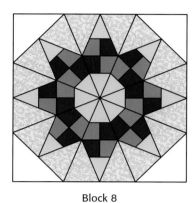

Block 8

TWO-COLOR DOUBLE-TIPPED CHECKERBOARD STAR: BLOCK 9

Repeat steps 1–9 of "Single-Color Double-Tipped Checkerboard Star: Block 8" on pages 33–35. Block 9 is made exactly as Block 8 except that you sew two different colors of 3½"-wide strips to the strip-set segments and arrange the pieced strips so that same colors are opposite each other.

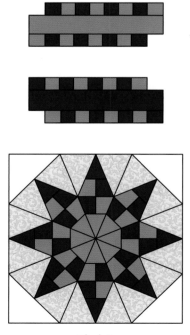

Block 9

CRAZY DAISY STAR: BLOCK 10 AND LIFESAVER STAR: BLOCK 11

1. *To make block 10,* sew three 3½" x 21" strips of fabric A and two 3½" x 21" strips of fabric B together along the long edges, alternating fabrics. Press the seams open. Crosscut the strip set into two segments, 7" wide, and two segments, 3" wide. Set aside the 3"-wide segments for block 11.

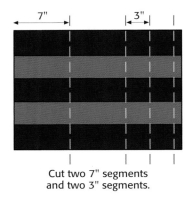

Cut two 7" segments and two 3" segments.

2. Stitch the 3½" x 15½" strip of fabric C between the two segments as shown. Sew the 3¼" x 15½" strips of fabric C to the top and bottom of the unit. Press the seams toward the C strips.

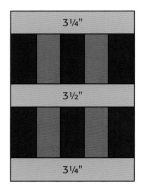

3. Lay the pieced unit on your cutting surface right side up as shown. Fold the bottom of the strip up so that the edge is just under the second seam line. Position the triangle ruler on the folded portion with the 4¾" line of the ruler at the fold and the centerline on the far left vertical seam line. Cut out the pieced diamond.

Repeat to cut one additional pieced diamond, repositioning the triangle ruler on the third vertical seam line from the left.

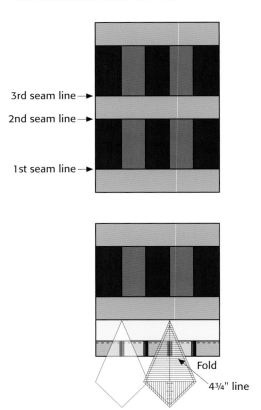

4. Refold the lower portion of the pieced unit so that the first horizontal seam line meets the third horizontal seam line. Position the triangle ruler on the second and fourth vertical seam lines as before and cut two additional pieced diamonds.

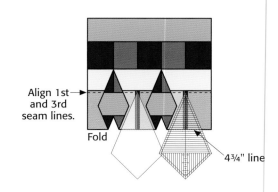

5. Cut four additional pieced diamonds from the opposite side of the pieced unit in the same manner.

6. Refer to "Basic Pieced Triangle Unit" on page 16 to sew two background triangles to each pieced diamond as shown.

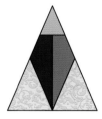

Make 8.

7. Refer to steps 2–7 of "Basic Star: Blocks 1 and 2" on pages 27 and 28 to sew the triangle units together as shown, add the corner triangles, and trim the block.

Block 10

8. *To make block 11,* sew the remaining 3½" x 21" strips of fabrics A and B together along the long edges, alternating colors as shown. Crosscut the strip set into two segments, 3" wide. From the remainder of the strip set, remove the stitching between one set of A and B strips. From the detached B strip, cut one rectangle, 3" x 3½", for use in step 10.

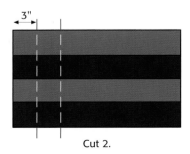

Cut 2.

9. Stitch each 3"-wide segment from step 8 to a 3"-wide segment that you set aside in step 1 as shown. Make two strips.

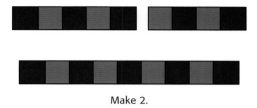

Make 2.

10. Remove an A piece from the beginning of one strip. Stitch the 3" x 3½" B rectangle from step 8 to the opposite end so that the strip begins and ends with a B piece.

Remove.　　　　　　　　　　　　　　　　Add.

11. Sew each 3" x 27½" C strip to one long edge of each strip-set segment as shown. Press the seams toward the C strips.

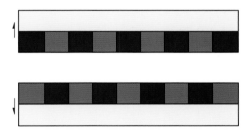

12. Lay the pieces from step 11 right sides together with the strip-set segments over the C strips. Stitch ¼" from the long edges. Refer to "Basic Pieced Triangle Unit" on page 16 to cut the pieced diamonds, placing the 4¾" line of the ruler on the seam and the ruler centerline on the strip set vertical seam lines. Cut eight pieced diamonds.

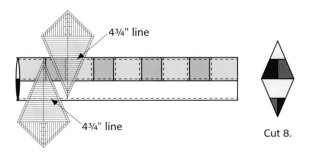

4¾" line

4¾" line

Cut 8.

13. Sew two background triangles to each pieced diamond as shown.

Make 8.

14. Refer to steps 2–7 of "Basic Star: Blocks 1 and 2" on pages 27 and 28 to sew the triangle units together as shown, add the corner triangles, and trim the block.

Block 11

TWIRLING STAR: BLOCK 12

1. Sew the two 3" x 21" strips together along the long edges. Press the seam open. From the strip set, cut four segments, 5¼" wide.

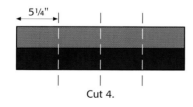

Cut 4.

2. Sew the segments together end to end as shown. Add the 3" x 5¼" rectangle to the end of the strip.

Add.

3. Layer the pieced strip and the 5¼" x 27½" strip right sides together. Sew ¼" from both long edges. Lay the strip on your cutting mat with the pieced strip face up. Refer to "Basic Pieced Triangle Unit" on page 16 to cut the pieced diamonds, placing the 4¾" line of the ruler on the seam and the ruler centerline on the strip-set vertical seam lines. Cut eight pieced diamonds.

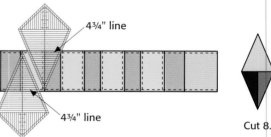

4¾" line

4¾" line

Cut 8.

4. Sew two background triangles to each pieced diamond as shown.

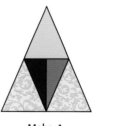 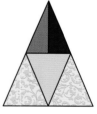

Make 4.   Make 4.

5. Refer to steps 2–7 of "Basic Star: Blocks 1 and 2" on pages 27 and 28 to sew the triangle units together as shown, add the corner triangles, and trim the block.

Block 12

CORNER STAR BLOCKS

1. Refer to "Background Triangles" on page 13 to cut 32 pairs of background triangles from the white 3¼" x 42" strips, placing the 3¼" line of the triangle ruler rather than the 5¼" line on the edge of the strip.

2. Refer to "Basic Pieced Triangle Unit" on page 16 to layer the assorted blue 3¼" x 42" strips together; stitch along both long edges. From the layered and stitched strip, cut 32 pieced diamonds, placing the 2¾" line of the triangle ruler on the seam lines and the 3" line on the strip edges. Cut as many pairs of diamonds as you can from the 42"-long strips. If you need more diamonds, layer, stitch, and cut the diamonds from the 8"-long strips in the same manner. Stitch two background triangles to each pieced diamond as shown. Trim the pieced diamonds, positioning the triangle ruler on the unit with the 2¾" line of the ruler on the horizontal seam line of the pieced diamond.

Make 16.   Make 16.

3. Refer to steps 2–7 of "Basic Star: Blocks 1 and 2" on pages 27 and 28 to sew the triangle units together as shown, add the corner triangles, and trim the blocks. Make four.

Make 4.

INNER PIECED BORDER

1. Lay two white 8½" x 42" strips right sides together. Make three pairs. From each of two pairs, cut two sets of trapezoids (eight total) and one set of end pieces (four total) as shown.

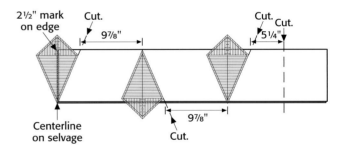

2. From the remaining pair, cut one set of trapezoids (two total) and two sets of end pieces (four total) as shown.

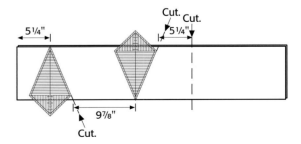

3. To make the inner side borders, stitch three trapezoids and one set of end pieces from step 2 and four large blue-and-yellow 45° triangles together as shown. Make two.

Side border.
Make 2.

4. To make the inner top and bottom borders, sew two trapezoids and one set of end pieces from step 2 and three large blue-and-yellow 45º triangles together as shown. Sew a Corner Star block to each end of the strip. Make two.

Top/bottom border.
Make 2.

ASSEMBLING THE QUILT TOP

1. Refer to the quilt assembly diagram on page 41 to arrange the blocks into four horizontal rows of three blocks each. The diagram shows the arrangement for the photographed quilt, but you can arrange the blocks any way you desire. Sew the blocks in each row together and then sew the rows together.

2. Stitch the inner side borders to the sides of the quilt top. Press the seams toward the border strips. Stitch the inner top and bottom borders to the top and bottom edges of the quilt top. Press the seams toward the border strips.

3. Sew two blue-and-yellow 2½" x 42" inner-border strips together end to end using a diagonal seam. Make four. From the pieced strips, cut two middle side border strips, 2½" x 80½", and two middle top/bottom border strips, 2½" x 64½".

4. Stitch the middle side borders to the sides of the quilt top. Press the seams toward the border strips. Sew a white 2½" square to each end of the top and bottom border strips. Stitch the strips to the top and bottom edges of the quilt top.

5. Sew two dark blue outer-border 5½" x 42" strips together end to end using a diagonal seam. Make four. From the pieced strips, cut two outer top/bottom border strips, 5½" x 68½". Stitch the excess from each strip to the two remaining pieced strips. From these strips, cut two outer side borders, 5½" x 84½".

6. Fold the remaining dark blue 5½" x 42" strip in half crosswise. Lay the triangle ruler on the strip with the 5½" line of the ruler along one long edge. Cut along both edges. Rotate the ruler so the 5½" line aligns with the opposite long edge and cut two more triangles. Continue in this manner to cut a total of four sets of triangles (eight total).

7. Sew the triangles together in pairs as shown. Make four. Stitch a pair to each end of each outer top and bottom border strip.

Make 4.

8. Sew the outer side borders to the sides of the quilt top. Press the seams toward the border strips. Sew the outer top and bottom borders to the top and bottom edges of the quilt top. Press the seams toward the border strips. Use a pizza pan or dinner plate to round the corners so they will be easier to bind.

FINISHING THE QUILT

Refer to "Techniques for Finishing" on page 89.

1. Layer the quilt top with batting and backing; baste.

2. Hand or machine quilt as desired.

3. Bind the quilt edges.

Quilt assembly

CRAZY DAISY CHAIN

Pieced by Mary Sue Suit. Quilted by Judy Woodworth.

*T*HIS QUILT IS an example of changing the look of a design by changing the blocks. I have used the same setting as for "Crazy Eights Sampler" on page 25, but it looks entirely different because I have used only the Crazy Daisy block instead of a variety of blocks. I created the chain effect by using two fabrics for the background triangles and two different fabrics for the block corners. The pieced inner border remains the same except that simple half-square triangle blocks are used in the corners instead of the Corner Star blocks. A pieced middle border is made from the same fabrics used in the Crazy Daisy blocks.

Finished quilt size: 78" x 94" • *Finished block size: 16" x 16"*

MATERIALS

Yardages are based on 42"-wide fabrics.

- 12 assorted fat quarters for block stars and pieced middle border
- 2⅜ yards of medium light colored fabric for block background triangles, block corners, and inner border
- 2⅛ yards of light colored fabric for block background triangles and inner border
- 1⅞ yards of fabric for inner-border corner squares and outer border
- 1 yard of multicolored fabric #1 for star centers
- 1 yard of multicolored fabric #2 for star centers
- ⅝ yard of medium colored fabric for block corners and inner-border corner squares
- 5½ yards of fabric for backing
- 1 yard of fabric for binding
- 82" x 98" piece of batting

CUTTING

All measurements include ¼"-wide seam allowances. Refer to "Cutting the Pieces" on page 13 for specifics on cutting the background triangles and large 45° triangles.

From *each* fat quarter, cut:
- 5 strips, 3½" x 21"

From multicolored fabric #1, cut:
- 6 strips, 3½" x 15½"
- 12 strips, 3¼" x 15½"

From multicolored fabric #2, cut:
- 6 strips, 3½" x 15½"
- 12 strips, 3¼" x 15½"

From the light colored fabric, cut:
- 9 strips, 5¼" x 42"; cut 72 sets of background triangles (144 total)
- 2 strips, 9" x 42"; cut 14 large 45° triangles

From the medium light colored fabric, cut:
- 3 strips, 5¼" x 42"; cut 24 sets of background triangles (48 total)
- 1 strip, 6" x 42"; crosscut into 6 squares, 6" x 6". Cut each square in half once diagonally to yield 12 triangles.
- 6 strips, 8½" x 42"

From the medium colored fabric, cut:
- 3 strips, 6" x 42"; crosscut into 18 squares, 6" x 6". Cut each square in half once diagonally to yield 36 triangles.
- 2 squares, 8⅞" x 8⅞"; cut each square in half once diagonally to yield 4 triangles

From the fabric for inner-border corner squares and outer border, cut:
- 9 strips, 5½" x 42"
- 2 squares, 8⅞" x 8⅞"; cut each square in half once diagonally to yield 4 triangles

PLANNING

1. Determine which two colors of fat quarters you will use for each Crazy Daisy Star. Each pair of colors will make two stars.

2. Refer to the illustration to decide where each star will be placed on the quilt top and number the pairs accordingly. This is important so that the correct background and corner pieces can be used to create the design. Note that pairs 1, 2, and 3 will use one multicolored fabric for the center of the star and pairs 4, 5, and 6 will use the other multicolored fabric.

Pair 1	Pair 4	Pair 2
Pair 5	Pair 3	Pair 6
Pair 6	Pair 3	Pair 5
Pair 2	Pair 4	Pair 1

MAKING THE BLOCKS

1. Using the predetermined pairs of fabrics, stitch three strips of one color and two of the other color from each pair together along the long edges. Repeat with the remaining strips from each pair. From each strip set, cut two 7"-wide segments. Set the remainder of each strip set aside for the middle pieced border.

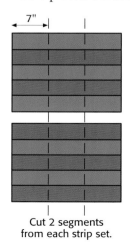

Cut 2 segments
from each strip set.

2. Refer to step 2 of "Crazy Daisy Star: Block 10 and Lifesaver Star: Block 11" on page 36 to stitch the 3½" x 15½" multicolored fabric strips between the two segments cut from each strip set; sew the 3¼" x 15½" multicolored fabric strips to the top and bottom of each segment. Use multicolored fabric #1 for pairs 1, 2, and 3 and multicolored fabric #2 for pairs 4, 5, and 6.

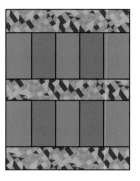

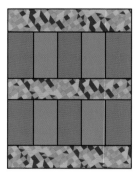

3. Place one pair of strip sets on your cutting surface so that one set is right side up and the other is wrong side up. Refer to steps 3–5 of "Crazy Daisy Star: Block 10 and Lifesaver Star: Block 11" on page 36 to cut the pieced diamonds from the strip sets.

4. To complete the pieced triangle units, stitch a light colored background triangle to the pieced diamonds from pairs 1, 2 and 3. Stitch a light colored background triangle to half of the pieced diamonds from pairs 4, 5, and 6. Stitch a medium light colored background triangle to the remaining pieced diamonds.

5. Refer to steps 2–7 of "Basic Star: Blocks 1 and 2" on pages 27 and 28 to sew the triangle units together as shown, add the corner triangles, and trim the blocks. Be careful to sew the correct color corner triangle to each pair of blocks.

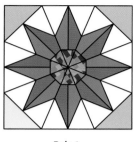

Pair 1.
Make 2.

Pair 2.
Make 2.

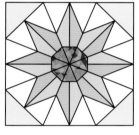

Pair 3.
Make 2.

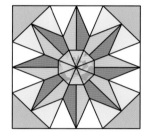

Pair 4.
Make 2.

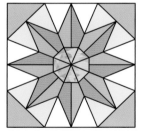

Pair 5.
Make 2.

Pair 6.
Make 2.

ASSEMBLING THE QUILT TOP

1. Refer to the quilt assembly diagram on page 46 and the pair placement diagram given previously to arrange the blocks into four horizontal rows of three blocks each as shown. Be careful to orient the corner blocks so the medium light colored corner triangle is pointing toward the inside of the quilt top. Sew the blocks in each row together and then sew the rows together.

2. Sew an 8⅞" medium colored triangle to each 8⅞" outer-border fabric triangle to make the inner-border corner squares.

Make 4.

3. Refer to steps 1–4 of "Inner Pieced Border" on pages 39–40 to assemble the inner pieced borders. Stitch the inner side borders to the sides of the quilt top. Sew the inner-border corner squares from step 2 to the top and bottom border strips and then sew the strips to the top and bottom edges of the quilt top.

4. To make the pieced middle border, cut the remainder of the strip sets into 2½"-wide segments. Stitch the segments together end to end as desired to make two side border strips, 64½" long, and two top/bottom border strips, 52½" long. Stitch the pieced middle side borders to the sides of the quilt top. Sew the middle top and bottom borders to the top and bottom edges of the quilt top.

5. Refer to steps 5–7 of "Assembling the Quilt Top" on page 40 to piece the outer borders and attach them to the quilt top.

Quilt assembly

DAISY CHAIN VARIATION.
Pieced and quilted by Mary Sue Suit.
The bold greens make the chain in this quilt more noticeable. The border treatment makes good use of left-over pieced diamonds.

FINISHING THE QUILT

Refer to "Techniques for Finishing" on page 89.

1. Layer the quilt top with batting and backing; baste.

2. Hand or machine quilt as desired.

3. Bind the quilt edges.

Neon Dragons

Pieced and quilted by Mary Sue Suit

I CALL THIS MY supersonic quilt because it is so easy to make. This particular quilt uses blocks 6 and 7, which are "buddy" stars: you get two different pieced diamonds from your strip set. The only way to make this quilt more quickly is to use block 1, the Basic Star.

When selecting fabrics, choose your border fabric first. It will be used for the stars and at the block corners as well. By using the same fabric for the border and corners, your stars will appear to shine through the "background sky" fabric. Just be sure you choose a background fabric that will show off the star points.

The stars are made from six fat quarters. You need two fat quarters to make each set of two blocks; each set includes one each of blocks 6 and 7. You will use the leftovers from the strip sets to make the border corner triangles and the binding.

Finished quilt size: 43" x 59" • *Finished block size: 16" x 16"*

MATERIALS

Yardages are based on 42"-wide fabrics.
- 6 assorted fat quarters for block stars, border corner triangles, and binding
- 1⅝ yards of fabric for block stars, block corners, and border
- 1⅛ yards of fabric for block backgrounds
- 3 yards of fabric for backing
- 47" x 63" piece of batting

CUTTING

From *each* fat quarter, cut:
- 2 strips, 5" x 21"

From the fabric for block stars, block corners, and border, cut:
- 3 strips, 2¾" x 42"
- 7 strips, 6" x 42"; crosscut 2 strips into 12 squares, 6" x 6". Cut each square in half once diagonally to yield 24 triangles. The remaining strips are for the border.

From the fabric for block backgrounds, cut:
- 6 strips, 5¼" x 42"; cut 48 sets of background triangles (96 total)

MAKING THE BLOCKS

1. Select two colors of fat-quarter 5" x 21" strips for each pair of stars (three sets).

2. Refer to "Single-Tipped Checkerboard Star: Block 6 and Stellar Buddy Star: Block 7" on pages 31–33 to construct the six blocks, one each of blocks 6 and 7 from *each* pair of fat quarters. Set the remainder of each strip set aside to make the border corner triangles.

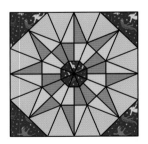

Block 6.
Make 3 total.

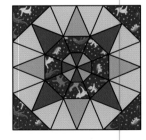

Block 7.
Make 3 total.

ASSEMBLING THE QUILT TOP

1. Refer to the quilt assembly diagram to arrange the blocks into three horizontal rows of two blocks each as desired. Don't worry about placement. Just let it happen.

2. Piece the remainder of the strip sets together to make a strip at least 5½" wide and at least 28" long. Be sure the long edges of the strip are even. Fold the strip in half crosswise. Lay the triangle ruler on the strip with the 6" line of the ruler along one long edge. Cut along both edges. Rotate the ruler so the 6" line aligns with the opposite long edge and cut two more triangles. Continue in this manner to cut a total of four sets of triangles (eight total). Stitch the triangles together in pairs. Make four.

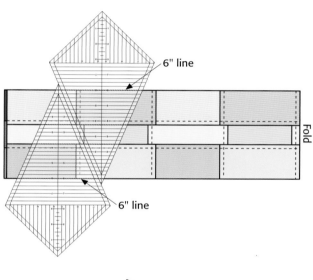

6" line

Fold

6" line

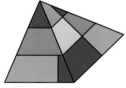

Make 4.

3. Sew two 6" x 42" strips together end to end using a diagonal seam. Make four. From the pieced strips, cut two top/bottom border strips, 6" x 32½", and two side border strips, 6" x 48½".

4. Stitch the side borders to the sides of the quilt top. Press the seams toward the borders. Sew a triangle pair to each end of the top and bottom border strips. Stitch the top and bottom border strips to the top and bottom edges of the quilt top. Press the seams toward the borders.

Quilt assembly

FINISHING THE QUILT

Refer to "Techniques for Finishing" on page 89.

1. Layer the quilt top with batting and backing; baste.

2. Hand or machine quilt as desired.

3. Sew the remainder of each fat quarter together to make a square approximately 24" x 24". Cut 2¼"-wide bias strips from the square and stitch them together end to end to make one long strip. Bind the quilt edges.

HEAVENLY HALOS

Pieced by Becky Umenthum. Quilted by Judy Woodworth.

Crown your blocks with a halo by adding an extra strip to each pieced triangle unit. The blocks in this quilt are all Squashed Basic Stars that use an assortment of blue fabrics. Each block is made just a bit bigger by adding the halo. For this quilt, Becky used two colors for the halos, but for a different effect, you could use just one color for all the blocks or a different color for each block. Halos that are uniform in color will create a more sophisticated tone. You really can't go wrong as long as you're getting the points.

Finished quilt size: 73" x 92" • *Finished block size: 19" x 19"*

MATERIALS

Yardages are based on 42"-wide fabrics.

- 3⅛ yards of fabric for block corners and border
- 2 yards *total* of assorted fabrics for block stars
- 2 yards of fabric for block backgrounds
- 1⅛ yards *each* of two different fabrics for halos and border corner triangles
- 5½ yards of fabric for backing
- 1 yard of fabric for binding
- 77" x 96" piece of batting

CUTTING

All measurements include ¼"-wide seam allowances. Refer to "Cutting the Pieces" on page 13 for specifics on cutting the background triangles.

From the assorted fabrics, cut:
- 24 strips, 5¼" x 21"

From the block background fabric, cut:
- 12 strips, 5¼" x 42"; cut 96 sets of background triangles (192 total)

From *each* halo and border-corner-triangle fabric, cut:
- 12 strips, 2" x 42"; crosscut into 48 strips, 2" x 10"
- 1 strip, 8½" x 21"

From the block corner and border fabric, cut:
- 5 strips, 7" x 42"; crosscut into 24 squares, 7" x 7". Cut each square in half once diagonally to yield 48 triangles.
- 8 strips, 8½" x 42"

MAKING THE BLOCKS

1. Select two assorted fabric strips for each block. Refer to steps 1 and 2 of "Squashed Basic Star: Block 3" on page 29 to cut eight pieced diamonds and make the pieced triangle units.

2. With right sides together, center a 2" x 10" strip on the short edge of each pieced triangle unit; stitch in place. Use the same color strip for the units of each block.

3. Use the triangle ruler to trim the ends of the strips even with the block sides, maintaining the angle.

4. Refer to steps 2–6 of "Basic Star: Blocks 1 and 2" on pages 27 and 28 to sew the triangle units together and add the corner triangles. Using a ruler that is at least 19½"

square, trim the blocks to 19½" x 19½", placing the 9¼" marks at the tip of the top diamond and the right side diamond. Trim any excess along the top and right side edges. Rotate the block 180° and repeat to trim the remaining two sides. You may also use a 12" ruler and trim each corner separately.

Make 6.   Make 6.

ASSEMBLING THE QUILT TOP

1. Refer to the quilt assembly diagram to arrange the blocks into four horizontal rows of three blocks each as desired. Sew the blocks in each row together and then sew the rows together.

2. Fold one of the 8½" x 21" border-corner-triangle strips in half crosswise. Lay the triangle ruler on the strip with the 2½" line on the 90° corner of the ruler along one long edge. Cut along both edges. Rotate the ruler so the same 2½" line aligns with the opposite long edge and cut two more triangles (four total). Repeat with the remaining 8½" x 21" strip.

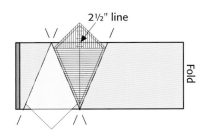

3. Sew one color of each triangle together in pairs. Make four pairs.

Make 4.

4. Sew two outer-border 8½" x 42" strips together end to end using a diagonal seam. Make four. From the pieced strips, cut two side border strips, 8½" x 76½", and two top/bottom border strips, 8½" x 57½".

5. Stitch the side border strips to the sides of the quilt top. Press the seams toward the borders. Sew a triangle pair to each end of the top and bottom border strips. Sew the strips to the top and bottom edges of the quilt top. Press the seams toward the borders.

Quilt assembly

FINISHING THE QUILT

Refer to "Techniques for Finishing" on page 89.

1. Layer the quilt top with batting and backing; baste.

2. Hand or machine quilt as desired.

3. Bind the quilt edges.

BASIC BEAUTY

Pieced by Mary Sue Suit. Quilted by Judy Woodworth.

THIS IS THE quilt that started the Crazy Eights idea. Created for a quilt retreat class, it inspired all the other projects in this book. This quilt is made up of twelve Basic Star blocks. I used white as the background and black for the corner triangles. The combination reminds me of the wonderful black-and-white tile floors I admire.

I have seen this quilt made in many fabric and color combinations, and all of them are great. No matter what your taste in fabric color and personality, the quilt will be fun to make and use. When choosing your fabric, just remember to ask yourself, "Will I get the points?" and it will be stellar.

Remember: you don't have to use just the Basic Star block. Make this a Star sampler or choose your favorite from those presented in "Crazy Eights Sampler" on page 25.

Finished quilt size: 74" x 90" • Finished block size: 16" x 16"

MATERIALS

Yardages are based on 42"-wide fabrics.

- ½ yard *each* of 8 assorted fabrics for block stars and pieced third border
- 4 yards of white fabric for block backgrounds, pieced first border, and pieced third border
- 4 yards of black fabric for block corners, pieced first border, second border, and fourth border
- 5½ yards of fabric for backing
- 1 yard of fabric for binding
- 78" x 94" piece of batting

CUTTING

All measurements include ¼"-wide seam allowances. Refer to "Cutting the Pieces" on page 13 for specifics on cutting the background triangles.

From *each* of the 8 assorted fabrics, cut:

- 2 strips, 5¼" x 42"

From the white fabric, cut:

- 16 strips, 5¼" x 42"; from 14 strips, cut 96 sets of background triangles (192 total)
- 7 strips, 5" x 42"
- 2 strips, 3½" x 42"
- 2 squares, 6" x 6"; cut each square in half once diagonally to yield 4 half-square triangles

From the black fabric, cut:

- 5 strips, 6" x 42"; crosscut into 26 squares, 6" x 6". Cut each square in half once diagonally to yield 52 half-square triangles.
- 4 squares, 10" x 10"; cut each square in half twice diagonally to make 16 quarter-square triangles
- 7 strips, 2½" x 42"
- 9 strips, 5½" x 42"

MAKING THE BLOCKS

1. Separate the 5¼" x 42" assorted fabric strips into four groups of two colors each.

2. Using one strip of each color from each group, refer to "Basic Star: Blocks 1 and 2" on page 27 to make a total of 12 blocks, using the black half-square triangles for the corners (you will have four left over for the borders). For the featured quilt, I arranged the pieced diamonds into the blocks shown below.

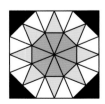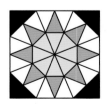

Make 12 blocks total.

ASSEMBLING THE QUILT TOP

1. Arrange the blocks into four horizontal rows of three blocks each as desired. Sew the blocks in each row together and then sew the rows together.

2. To make the pieced first border, fold the white 5" x 42" strip in half crosswise. Cut the ends at a 45° angle. Measure 6¾" across the top edge and make a mark. Position the 45° angle of the ruler at the bottom of the strip and cut across the strip on the opposite diagonal as the first cut. Open up the strip to see if there is enough to cut one additional trapezoid. Repeat the procedure with the remaining strips to cut a total of 14 trapezoids. If you can cut three trapezoids from each strip, you will only need five strips.

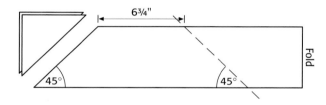

3. To make the first side-border strips, stitch four trapezoids and three black quarter-square triangles together as shown. Stitch a black half-square triangle to the ends of the strip. Make two. To make the first top/bottom border strips, stitch three trapezoids and four black quarter-square triangles together as shown. Stitch a white half-square triangle to the ends of the strip. Make two.

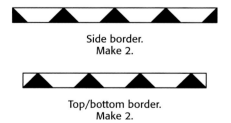

Side border.
Make 2.

Top/bottom border.
Make 2.

4. Refer to the quilt assembly diagram on page 56 to stitch the first side borders to the sides of the quilt top, aligning the triangles on the border strips with the triangles that form from the block corners to create squares. Press the seams toward the borders. Stitch the first top/bottom borders to the top and bottom edges of the quilt top in the same manner. Press the seams toward the borders.

5. For the second border, stitch the 2½" x 42" black strips together end to end to make one long strip. From the pieced strip, cut two side borders, 73½" long, and two top/bottom borders, 61½" long.

6. Stitch the second side borders to the sides of the quilt top. Press the seams toward the borders. Stitch the second top and bottom borders to the top and bottom edges of the quilt top. Press the seams toward the borders.

7. To make the pieced third border, cut four trapezoids from the 3½" x 42" white strips as shown.

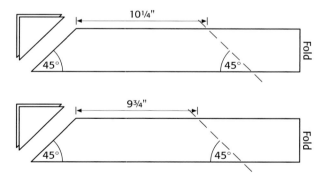

8. Cut a total of 28 pieced diamonds from the remainder of the strip sets. To create the checkerboard diamonds shown in the featured quilt, remove the stitching from the end pieces and sew them together again as shown. Lay your triangle ruler on each of the two new pieces with the 5¼" line of the ruler at the base of the pieces; cut the new triangle piece. Stitch the two triangles together to make a pieced diamond. This is a great way to use your leftovers and create interest in the quilt, but any pieced diamond from any block in this book could also

be cut from leftovers of the assorted fabrics and used in the border.

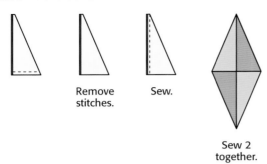

Remove stitches.

Sew.

Sew 2 together.

9. Lay two of the remaining 5¼" x 42" white strips right sides together. Stitch ¼" from both long edges. Make two. From the layered strips, cut 28 pieced diamonds.

10. To make the third top and bottom border strips, stitch one 10¼" trapezoid from step 7, six pieced colored diamonds from step 8, and six pieced white diamonds from step 9 together as shown. To make the third side borders, stitch one 9¾" trapezoid, eight colored diamonds, and eight white diamonds together as shown. You can change the placement of the trapezoid within the strips as desired.

Top/bottom border.
Make 2.

Side border.
Make 2.

11. Stitch the third side borders to the sides of the quilt top. Press the seams toward the second border. Stitch the third top and bottom borders to the top and bottom edges of the quilt top. Press the seams toward the second border.

12. To make the fourth border, sew two black 5½" x 42" strips together end to end using a diagonal seam. Make four. From the pieced strips, cut two side border strips, 5½" x 73½", and two top/bottom border strips, 5½" x 61½".

13. Fold the remaining 5½" x 42" black strips in half crosswise. Lay the triangle ruler on the strip with the 5½" line of the ruler along one long edge. Cut along both edges. Rotate the ruler so the 5½" line aligns with the opposite long edge and cut two more triangles. Repeat to cut a total of eight triangles.

14. Sew the triangles together in pairs. Make four.

Make 4.

15. Stitch the side border strips to the sides of the quilt top. Press the seams toward the borders. Sew a triangle pair to each end of the top and bottom border strips. Sew the strips to the top and bottom edges of the quilt top. Press the seams toward the borders.

Quilt assembly

FINISHING THE QUILT

Refer to "Techniques for Finishing" on page 89.

1. Layer the quilt top with batting and backing; baste.

2. Hand or machine quilt as desired.

3. Bind the quilt edges.

Cherry Seven-Up

Pieced and quilted by Mary Sue Suit

*T*HIS IS MY first attempt at working with reproduction fabrics. I fell in love with the yellow polka-dot fabric and had to have it. It is part of a "forties" collection that included the green polka-dots (also a must), so what could I do but purchase companion pieces and have fun?

You will notice that several points of the corner stars blend with and become part of the inner checkerboard element of the design. To accomplish this, I used the dark polka-dot fabrics and the medium-scale print fabrics of the corresponding colors. Using medium-scale prints of differing colors would allow you to get the points if that is what you desire.

Finished quilt size: 76" x 92" • Finished block size: 16" x 16"

MATERIALS

Yardages are based on 42"-wide fabrics.

- 2⅞ yards of rose print for block corners, pieced inner border, and outer border
- 1¾ yards of bright green polka-dot for block stars and pieced middle border
- 1¾ yards of bright yellow polka-dot for block stars and pieced middle border
- 1¾ yards of off-white fabric for block backgrounds
- 1 yard of off-white print for block backgrounds and pieced inner border
- ⅞ yard of medium yellow print for blocks
- ⅞ yard of medium-scale green print for blocks
- 5½ yards of fabric for backing
- 1 yard of fabric for binding
- 80" x 96" piece of batting

CUTTING

All measurements include ¼"-wide seam allowances. Refer to "Cutting the Pieces" on page 13 for specifics on cutting the background triangles.

From the bright green polka-dot, cut:
- 6 strips, 2¾" x 42"
- 3 strips, 3½" x 42"
- 8 strips, 2½" x 42"
- 2 squares, 5" x 5"

From the bright yellow polka-dot, cut:
- 6 strips, 2¾" x 42"
- 3 strips, 3½" x 42"
- 8 strips, 2½" x 42"
- 2 squares, 5" x 5"

From the off-white fabric, cut:
- 3 strips, 5¼" x 42"; cut 20 sets of background triangles (40 total)
- 6 strips, 5¼" x 42"; crosscut 3 strips into 6 rectangles, 5¼" x 16½". The remaining strips will be used to cut the trapezoids.
- 1 strip, 6" x 42"; crosscut into 4 squares, 6" x 6"

From the off-white print, cut:
- 2 strips, 5¼" x 42"; cut 16 sets of background triangles (32 total)
- 6 strips, 2½" x 42"
- 2 squares, 5" x 5"

From the medium yellow print, cut:
- 1 strip, 5¼" x 42"; cut 6 sets of background triangles (12 total)
- 4 strips, 4½" x 24"

From the medium green print, cut:
- 1 strip, 5¼" x 42"; cut 6 sets of background triangles (12 total)
- 4 strips, 4½" x 24"

From the rose print, cut:

- 8 strips, 6½" x 42"
- 2 strips, 6" x 42"; crosscut into 10 squares, 6" x 6". Cut each square in half once diagonally to yield 20 triangles.
- 1 strip, 5¾" x 42"; crosscut into 6 squares, 5¾" x 5¾". Cut each square in half once diagonally to yield 12 triangles.
- 6 strips, 2½" x 42"
- 2 squares, 5" x 5"

MAKING THE BLOCKS

1. Refer to "Two-Color Double-Tipped Checkerboard Star: Block 9" on page 35 to stitch the bright green polka-dot and bright yellow polka-dot 2¾" x 42" strips together to make three strip sets. Cut each strip set in half and stitch the two halves together side by side. From the strip sets, cut 24 segments, 2¼" wide. Stitch the 3½" x 42" strips to these segments and cut the pieced diamonds. Use the appropriate color background triangles and the rose and off-white triangles for the block corners to make six blocks as shown.

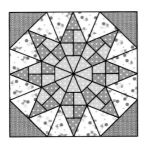

Make 2.

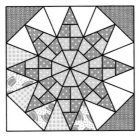

Make 4.

2. To make the alternate blocks, cut six trapezoids from the remaining off-white 5¼" x 42" strips as shown.

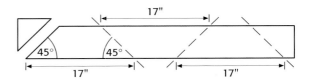

3. With right sides together and the bottom edges even, stitch a 5¾" rose print triangle to each end of each trapezoid. Press the seams toward the triangles. Make six units.

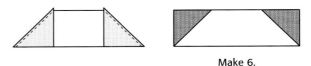

Make 6.

4. Stitch two 4½" x 24" medium yellow and medium green strips together, alternating the colors as shown. Make two strip sets. Press the seams in one direction. Crosscut the strip sets into 12 segments, 3¾" wide.

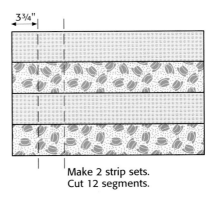

Make 2 strip sets.
Cut 12 segments.

5. Sew two segments together as shown. Make six units.

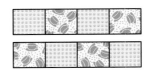 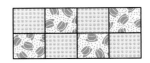

Make 6.

6. Stitch one unit from step 3, one unit from step 5, and one 5¼" x 16½" off-white rectangle together as shown. Make six blocks.

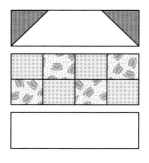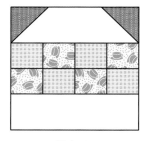

Make 6.

ASSEMBLING THE QUILT TOP

1. Arrange the blocks into four horizontal rows, rotating the blocks as shown to achieve the design. Stitch the blocks in each row together and then stitch the rows together.

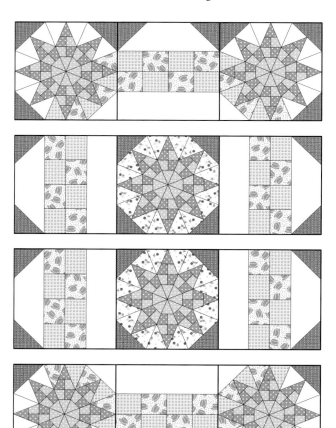

2. To make the pieced inner border, stitch the 2½" x 42" off-white print strips together end to end to make one long strip. Repeat with the 2½" x 42" rose print strips. Stitch the pieced strips together along one long edge. From the pieced strip, cut two side border strips, 64½" long, and two top/bottom border strips, 48½" long.

3. Lay one 5" off-white print square and one 5" rose print square right sides together. Stitch ¼" from two opposite edges. Cut the pair in half to create two segments, 2½" wide. With the segments placed so that the seam is horizontal, layer these two segments right sides together so opposite colors face each other. Stitch ¼" from the left and right edges. Cut the pair in half again to create two checkerboard squares. Repeat to make two additional squares.

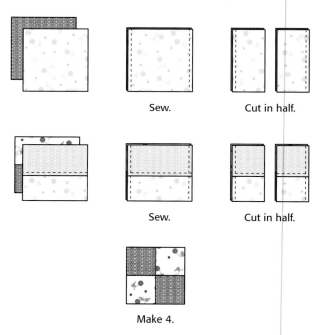

Sew.   Cut in half.

Sew.   Cut in half.

Make 4.

4. Stitch the pieced inner side borders to the sides of the quilt top. Press the seams toward the borders. Sew a checkerboard square from step 3 to each end of each top and bottom border strip so that the colors in the squares alternate with the colors in the strips. Stitch these strips to the top and bottom edges of the quilt top. Press the seams toward the borders.

5. To make the pieced middle border, stitch each 2½" x 42" bright green polka-dot strip to a 2½" x 42" bright yellow polka-dot strip. Make eight strip sets. Crosscut the strip sets into 64 segments, 4½" wide.

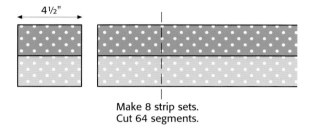

← 4½" →

Make 8 strip sets.
Cut 64 segments.

6. Stitch the segments together in pairs as shown. Make 32.

Make 32.

7. To make the middle side borders, stitch nine units from step 6 together as shown. Make two. For the middle top and bottom borders, stitch seven units together as shown. Make two.

8. Refer to step 3 to make four checkerboard blocks, using the 5" bright green polka-dot and bright yellow polka-dot squares.

9. Stitch the middle side borders to the sides of the quilt top. Press the seams toward the inner border. Sew a checkerboard block from step 8 to each end of the top and bottom border strips. Stitch the strips to the top and bottom edges of the quilt top. Press the seams toward the inner border.

10. To make the outer border, sew seven 6½" x 42" rose strips together end to end to make one long strip. From the strip, cut two side border strips, 80½" long, and two top/bottom border strips, 64½" long.

11. Fold the remaining 6½" x 42" rose strip in half crosswise. Lay the triangle ruler on the strip with the 6½" line of the ruler along one long edge. Cut along both edges. Rotate the ruler so the 6½" line aligns with the opposite long edge and cut two more triangles. Repeat to cut a total of eight triangles.

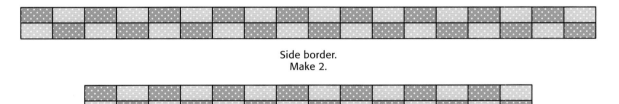

Side border.
Make 2.

Top/bottom border.
Make 2.

Tip

Make a checkerboard block using two trapezoid units. Add a Star block to each side to make a fast table runner.

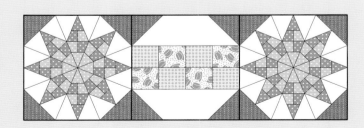

12. Sew the triangles together in pairs. Make four.

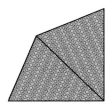

Make 4.

13. Stitch the side border strips to the sides of the quilt top. Press the seams toward the borders. Sew a triangle pair to each end of the top and bottom border strips. Sew the strips to the top and bottom edges of the quilt top. Press the seams toward the borders.

FINISHING THE QUILT

Refer to "Techniques for Finishing" on page 89.

1. Layer the quilt top with batting and backing; baste.

2. Hand or machine quilt as desired.

3. Bind the quilt edges.

Quilt assembly

LIME SURPRISE

Pieced by Mary Sue Suit and Judy Woodworth. Quilted by Judy Woodworth.

W HAT CAN I SAY? It just happened! I collaborated with Judy Woodworth, who did the machine quilting for most of the quilts in this book, before the overall design for this quilt was established. Judy started the center star and I finished it once I knew what the design would be. I am sure she will agree that this quilt was quite a surprise when she saw it, but I got the points.

The design of this quilt allows the star to explode through the checkerboard border surrounding it. Believe it or not, it is deceptively easy to put together and so much fun you won't believe it.

If you want, just make the center star. It finishes to 32" square. Use it by itself or as the basis for a medallion design of your own. Add pieced triangle units to four sides to create the exploded star medallion, which finishes to 64" square. It's smashing on a table or put diagonally across any size bed. Set on top of a plain bedspread, it will change the mood of the room without having to be a large quilt. The size of your universe is up to you and your needs.

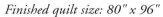

Finished quilt size: 80" x 96"

NOTE: *Due to a quiltmaker error (mine), your center star will differ slightly from the photo on page 63. If you follow the quilt assembly diagram, your center star will be correct.*

MATERIALS

Yardages are based on 42"-wide fabrics.

- 3⅝ yards of dark colored print for center medallion corners, checkerboard border, and outer border
- 3 yards of light colored print for block backgrounds
- 1⅜ yards of dark purple fabric for block stars, pieced triangle units, and checkerboard border
- 1⅛ yards of fuchsia fabric for narrow borders
- 1 yard of medium blue batik for block stars and pieced triangle units
- ⅞ yard of lime green fabric for center medallion background
- ⅝ yard of bright pink fabric for center star background and pieced triangle units
- 1 yard of fabric for binding
- 6 yards of fabric for backing
- 84" x 100" piece of batting

CUTTING

All measurements include ¼"-wide seam allowances. Refer to "Cutting the Pieces" on page 13 for specifics on cutting the background triangles and the large 45° triangles.

From the dark purple fabric, cut:
- 3 strips, 5" x 42"
- 4 strips, 5¼" x 42"

From the medium blue batik, cut:
- 3 strips, 5" x 42"
- 4 strips, 5¼" x 42"

From the bright pink fabric, cut:
- 3 strips, 5¼" x 42"; cut 24 sets of background triangles (48 total)

From the lime green fabric, cut:
- 3 strips, 9" x 42"; cut 24 large 45° triangles

From the dark colored print, cut:

- 10 strips, 8½" x 42"; cut 2 strips into 4 rectangles, 8½" x 16½"
- 2 strips, 6" x 42"; crosscut into 8 squares, 6" x 6". Cut each square in half once diagonally to yield 16 half-square triangles.
- 2 strips, 5" x 42"
- 2 squares, 10⅞" x 10⅞"; cut each square in half once diagonally to yield 4 half-square triangles

From the fuchsia fabric, cut:

- 8 strips, 2½" x 42"
- 1 strip, 9" x 14"; cut 2 large 45° triangles
- 2 squares, 6" x 6"; cut each square in half once diagonally to yield 4 half-square triangles

From the light colored print, cut:

- 1 strip, 9" x 42"; cut 8 large 45° triangles
- 8 strips, 5¼" x 42"; cut 64 sets of background triangles (128 total)
- 8 strips, 4½" x 42"
- 2 squares, 6" x 6"; cut each square in half once diagonally to yield 4 half-square triangles

MAKING THE CENTER STAR

1. Stitch a 5" x 42" dark purple strip and a 5" x 42" medium blue batik strip together along the long edges. Make three. Crosscut the strip sets into 16 segments, 5¼" wide.

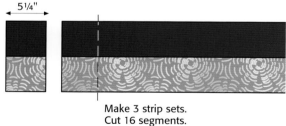

Make 3 strip sets.
Cut 16 segments.

2. Sew four segments together side by side as shown. Make four.

Make 4.

3. Layer two pieced strips from step 2 right sides together so that opposite fabrics face each other. Sew ¼" from all four sides.

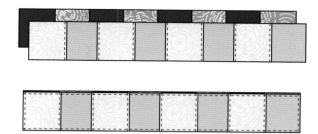

Sew together on all four sides.

4. Lay the triangle ruler on the layered strip sets with the 4¾" line on the bottom horizontal seam and the ruler centerline on the far left strip-set seam; cut the triangle. The triangles cut on the strip-set seams will be checkerboard triangles. Lay the ruler on the opposite horizontal seam line and between the strip-set seams; cut the plain pieced triangle. Continue in this manner to cut eight plain pieced triangles and seven checkerboard triangles. Set the end pieces aside.

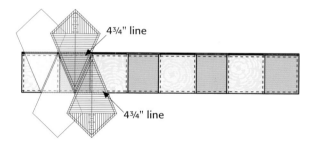

4¾" line

4¾" line

5. Repeat steps 3 and 4 with the remaining pieced strips. You now have 16 plain pieced triangles and 14 checkerboard triangles.

Cut 16.   Cut 14.

6. Rip out the horizontal lines of stitching on the end pieces that you set aside. Press open the pieces with an iron to reveal half of a checkerboard triangle. Stitch two triangles together along the short edges. Use the triangle ruler to trim the triangle to the correct size. Make two.

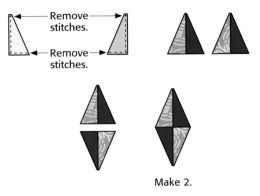

Make 2.

7. Sew the bright pink background triangles to eight of the plain pieced diamonds and all of the checkerboard diamonds as shown. Set the remaining plain pieced diamonds aside for the checkerboard border.

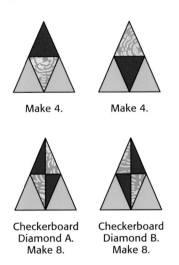

Make 4.　Make 4.

Checkerboard Diamond A. Make 8.　Checkerboard Diamond B. Make 8.

8. Stitch a checkerboard triangle unit to each plain triangle unit as shown. Stitch the remaining checkerboard units to each other as shown.

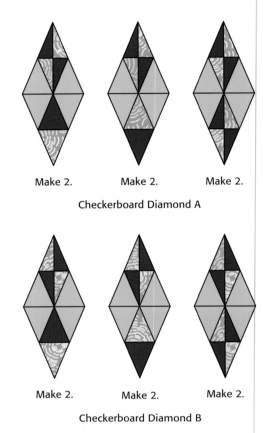

Make 2.　Make 2.　Make 2.

Checkerboard Diamond A

Make 2.　Make 2.　Make 2.

Checkerboard Diamond B

9. Sew a lime green 45° triangle to each diamond unit from step 7. For the units with plain pieced diamonds, sew the triangles to the sides of the checkerboard diamond half. Place a long ruler along the edge of the trimmed background triangles to trim the sides of the larger triangle units.

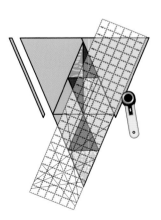

10. To trim the short edge of the triangle units, lay your long ruler on the triangle with the ¼" line of the ruler at the pieced triangle tip. Trim any excess above the ruler.

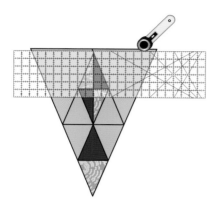

11. Stitch the eight triangle units with plain pieced triangles together as shown. Set the remaining triangles aside for the checkerboard border.

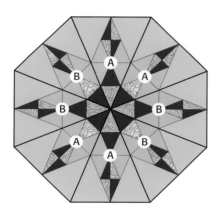

12. Sew the dark print half-square triangles that were cut from the 10⅞" squares to the corners of the octagon as shown. Square up the block.

MAKING AND ADDING THE CHECKERBOARD BORDER

1. Sew the 5" x 42" dark purple and dark print strips together along the long edge, alternating colors. Press the seams in one direction. Cut the strip set in half crosswise and sew the two sections together side by side as shown.

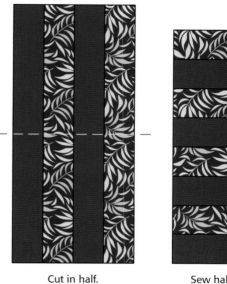

Cut in half.   Sew halves together.

2. Crosscut the strip set into eight segments, 2½" wide.

2½"

Cut 8 segments.

3. Sew two segments together as shown. Make four.

Make 4.

4. Sew a 2½" x 42" fuchsia strip to each 4½" x 42" light print strip. Press the seam toward the fuchsia strip. Make eight. Sew these pieced strips to the top and bottom of each checkerboard strip from step 3 as shown, keeping the ends even on one end.

Make 4.

5. Fold each strip set in half, right sides together, and lightly crease along the fold to mark the center of the strip. Open the strips back up.

6. For each strip set, place the triangle ruler on the unit with the ruler centerline on the strip-set creased centerline and the tip of the ruler at the bottom of the pieced unit as shown. Cut along the right edge of the ruler, sliding the ruler up to make the full cut. Repeat on the opposite side to complete the cutting.

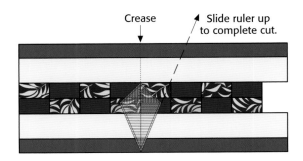

Crease · Slide ruler up to complete cut.

7. Measure 10" from the short edge of each piece; trim the excess. Set the excess aside for use later.

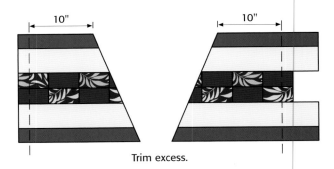

Trim excess.

8. Sew a checkerboard unit to each side of a large pieced triangle unit that you set aside from the center star as shown. Make four.

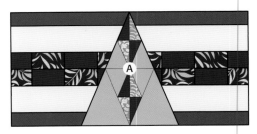

Make 2.

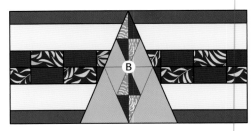

Make 2.

9. Refer to "Basic Pieced Triangle Unit" on page 16 to sew each 5¼" x 42" dark purple strip to a 5¼" x 42" medium blue batik strip. Cut a total of 56 pieced diamonds. Sew two light print background triangles to each pieced diamond that you cut here, plus the eight diamonds that you set aside in the center star instructions, to complete the triangle units.

Make 32.   Make 32.

10. Refer to the block 2 instructions of "Basic Star: Blocks 1 and 2" on page 29 to stitch eight triangle units together, as shown, to make an octagon. Do not stitch the corners to the blocks. Make eight. Set four aside for the outer border.

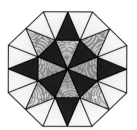

Make 8.

11. Remove the checkerboard portion from the leftover strip-set pieces that you set aside in step 7. From the fuchsia/light print segments, cut eight 6½" squares. Place two squares right sides together with the same fabrics facing. Make four pairs. Stitch ¼" from one edge of each pair as shown. Cut the pairs in half diagonally as shown. Each pair will yield two loose triangles and a piece that is stitched together.

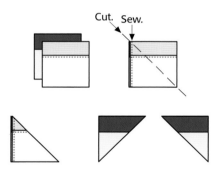

12. Stitch the two loose triangles from each pair to opposite corners of the four star octagons as shown. Stitch a dark print half-square triangle to one of the remaining corners of each octagon as shown.

13. Cut ¼" off the diagonal edge of each of the stitched-together pieces from step 11.

Trim ¼".

14. Press the triangles open. Lay your long ruler on the triangle with the 2⅜" line of the ruler on the seam between the two colors as shown. Cut along the lower edge of the ruler, and discard the trimmed portion.

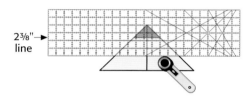

2⅜" line

15. Stitch the trimmed triangle to the remaining corner of each of the octagons, as shown, to complete the blocks.

Make 4.

16. Refer to the quilt assembly diagram on page 72 to stitch a unit from step 8 to each side of the center Star block. Stitch the blocks from step 15 to the ends of the remaining two units and stitch them to the top and bottom of the block.

MAKING AND ADDING THE OUTER BORDER

1. Refer to steps 6 and 7 of "Basic Star: Blocks 1 and 2" on page 28 to add three dark print 6" triangles and one fuchsia 6" triangle to the corners of the remaining octagons, as shown, to complete the Star blocks for the outer border. Make four.

Make 4.

2. Stitch the blocks together in pairs as shown.

Make 2.

3. Fold two 8½" x 42" dark print strips in half crosswise. *On each strip,* make a mark 5¼" from the end of the lower edge. Place your triangle ruler on the strip with the tip on the mark as shown. Cut along the right side of the ruler to create one set of small end pieces. Measure 5¼" from the angled cut at the top of the strip and make a straight vertical cut, as shown, to create one additional set of end pieces. You should have a total of four sets of small end pieces.

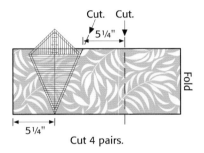

Cut 4 pairs.

4. Fold the remaining two 8½" x 42" strips in half crosswise. *On each strip,* lay the triangle ruler centerline on the raw edges of the strip unfolded end. Cut along the right side of the ruler. Measure 13¼" from the upper edge of the angled cut and make a mark. Place your straight ruler on the strip with the right edge on the mark as shown. Cut along the right side of the ruler to create two large end pieces (four total).

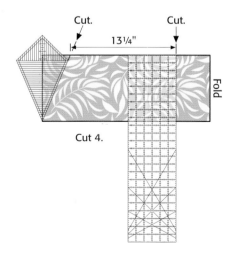

Cut 4.

5. Stitch one set of small end pieces to four light print large 45° triangles as shown. Stitch a dark print 8½" x 16½" rectangle to the top of each unit. Make four.

Make 4.

6. Stitch a unit from step 5 to each side of the block pairs as shown. Refer to the quilt assembly diagram to stitch these units to the top and bottom of the quilt top.

Make 2.

7. Cut one trapezoid from each of four of the 8½" x 42" dark print strips as shown.

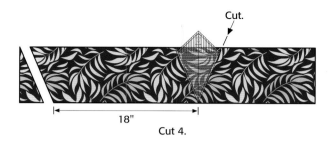

18"

Cut 4.

8. From the remainder of the strips, cut eight corner triangles, aligning the 2½" line on the 90° corner of the ruler with the edge of the strip.

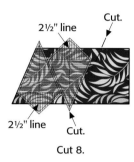

Cut 8.

9. Stitch the corner triangles together in pairs. Make four.

Make 4.

10. Stitch two end pieces, two trapezoids, two light print large 45° triangles, and one fuchsia large 45° triangle together as shown. Sew a corner triangle pair to each end of the strip. Make two. Refer to the quilt assembly diagram to stitch the strips to the sides of the quilt top.

Make 2.

FINISHING THE QUILT

Refer to "Techniques for Finishing" on page 89.

1. Layer the quilt top with batting and backing; baste.

2. Hand or machine quilt as desired.

3. Bind the quilt edges.

Quilt assembly

Holiday Topper

Pieced by Mary Sue Suit. Quilted by Judy Woodworth.

I CALL THIS A topper quilt because when placed on top of a plain bedspread, it is just the right size to top off a double bed and give the guest room a holiday look. It is also large enough to "top off" anyone lounging in the recliner.

This quilt design is fat-quarter friendly, so expansion is easy. It is no problem to top off any bed size or lounging giant (or elf). Only the border and background batik fabrics require more than a fat quarter. Remember to choose varied color values in order to see the diamonds within rectangles within diamonds.

Finished quilt size: 68" x 80" · Finished block size: 6½" x 16"

MATERIALS

Yardages are based on 42"-wide fabrics.
- 2½ yards of fabric for border and binding
- 1½ yards of multicolored batik for background
- 1 fat quarter *each* of 4 medium golds
- 1 fat quarter *each* of 3 dark reds
- 1 fat quarter *each* of 3 dark greens
- 1 fat quarter *each* of 2 medium reds
- 1 fat quarter *each* of 2 medium greens
- 1 fat quarter *each* of 2 dark golds
- 4 yards of fabric for backing
- 72" x 84" piece of batting

CUTTING

All measurements include ¼"-wide seam allowances. Refer to "Cutting the Pieces" on page 13 for specifics on cutting the large 45° triangles.

From *each* of the dark red fat quarters, cut:
- 1 rectangle, 8" x 18"

From *each* of 2 of the dark red fat quarters, cut:
- 1 strip, 5¼" x 21"

From *each* of the medium red fat quarters, cut:
- 1 strip, 5¼" x 21"

From 1 of the medium red fat quarters, cut:
- 4 rectangles, 4½" x 9"

From the other medium red fat quarter, cut:
- 2 rectangles, 4½" x 9"

From *each* of the dark green fat quarters, cut:
- 1 rectangle, 8" x 18"

From 2 of the dark green fat quarters, cut:
- 1 strip, 5¼" x 21"

From *each* of the medium green fat quarters, cut:
- 1 strip, 5¼" x 21"

From 1 of the medium green fat quarters, cut:
- 4 rectangles, 4½" x 9"

From the other medium green fat quarter, cut:
- 2 rectangles, 4½" x 9"

From *each* of the medium gold fat quarters, cut:
- 1 rectangle, 8" x 18"

From 2 of the medium gold fat quarters, cut:
- 1 strip, 5¼" x 21"

From *each* of the dark gold fat quarters, cut:
- 4 rectangles, 4½" x 9"

From 2 of the dark gold fat quarters, cut:
- 1 strip 5¼" x 21"

From the multicolored batik, cut:

- 1 strip, 9" x 21"; cut 4 large 45° triangles
- 2 strips, 8½" x 42"
- 3 strips, 3¾" x 42"; crosscut into:
  - 4 rectangles, 3¾" x 16½"
  - 4 rectangles, 3¾" x 8½"
- 2 rectangles, 8" x 18"
- 2 rectangles, 4½" x 9"

From the border fabric, cut:

- 8 strips, 6½" x 42"

MAKING THE BLOCKS

1. Refer to "Basic Pieced Triangle Unit" on page 16 to layer each dark red 5¼" x 21" strip with a medium red 5¼" x 21" strip. Cut eight pieced diamonds from one pair and six pieced diamonds from the other pair. Repeat with one dark green and one medium green 5¼" x 21" strip to cut six pieced diamonds.

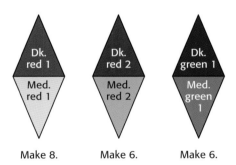

Make 8.   Make 6.   Make 6.

2. Refer to "Background Triangles" on page 13 to cut background triangles from the remaining medium green, dark green, medium gold, and dark gold 5¼" x 21" strips. Cut four sets (eight total) from *each* green strip. Cut four sets (eight total) *each* from one dark gold and one medium gold strip. Cut two sets (four total) from the remaining dark gold and medium gold strips. You should have a total of 40 background triangles.

3. Refer to "Basic Pieced Triangle Unit" on page 16 to sew the background triangles to the pieced diamonds as shown.

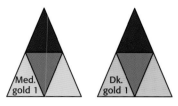

Make 3 each.

Make 4 each.

Make 3 each.

4. Refer to "90° Triangles" on page 14 to use method 2 to cut two 90° triangles from each 4½" x 9" fat quarter and batik rectangle.

5. Stitch the fat-quarter 90° triangles to the sides of the basic pieced triangle units as shown. Trim the units to 7" x 8½". Set the batik 90° triangles aside for later.

Dark gold 1 →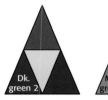← Dark gold 2

Make 2 each.

Med. red 1 →← Med. red 2

Make 2 each.   Make 1 each.

Med. green 2 →← Med. green 1

Make 2 each.   Make 1 each.

6. Sew the units from step 5 together as shown. Trim the blocks to 7" x 16½".

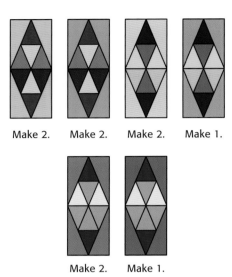

Make 2.   Make 2.   Make 2.   Make 1.

Make 2.   Make 1.

7. Refer to "Double Lunatic Fringe Block" on page 19 to cut the fat quarter 8" x 18" rectangles apart. Stitch the pieces together as shown to make one of each of the blocks shown, using the batik 45° triangles where shown. Trim the blocks to 7" x 16½".

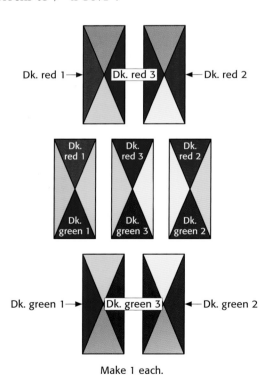

Make 1 each.

8. Mark ¼" from opposite ends of the two 8" x 18" batik rectangles as shown. Cut the rectangles in half diagonally from mark to mark.

9. Sew the half rectangles from step 8 and the appropriate remaining side and 45° triangles together to make one of each of the blocks shown. Trim the blocks to 7" x 16½".

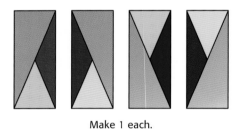

Make 1 each.

10. Fold the remaining gold side triangles in half; lightly crease them to mark the centers. Open up the triangles. Place the 8½" line of your long ruler on the center mark of one triangle; cut off the tip that extends beyond the ruler. Repeat on the opposite side of the triangle. Trim the remaining triangle in the same manner.

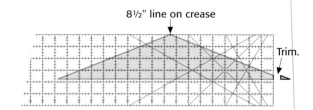

11. Lay one of the batik 90° triangles that you set aside earlier on one short side of each trimmed triangle, right sides together; stitch. Repeat on the opposite short side. Make two.

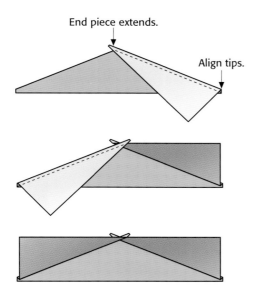

12. Trim the blocks to 3¾" x 16½". To trim the block evenly, place it horizontally on the cutting surface. Lay your long ruler on the block with the 8¼" vertical line of the ruler through the center of the triangle and the ¼" horizontal line of the ruler at the tip of the triangle. Trim along the right and top edges. Repeat on the opposite end of the blocks.

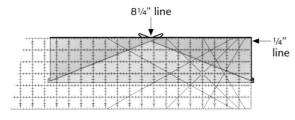

Trim top and side edges.

13. Place the 3¾" horizontal line of the ruler along the top edge of the block. Trim the bottom edge. These are the blocks for the ends of row 3.

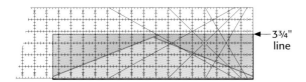

Trim bottom edge.

14. Fold each batik 8½" x 42" strip in half crosswise. *For each strip,* mark 6¾" from the left bottom edge. Lay your triangle ruler on the strip with the tip on the mark as shown. Cut along the right edge of the ruler to create one set of end pieces. Mark 6¾" from the top of the angled cut. Lay your triangle ruler on the strip with the left edge at the mark. Cut along the left edge of the ruler to make two trapezoids.

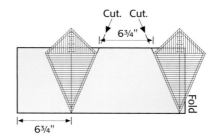

ASSEMBLING THE QUILT TOP

1. Arrange the blocks as shown to make the five rows. Stitch the pieces in each row together. Sew rows 1 and 2 together and rows 4 and 5 together. Stitch a batik 3¾" x 24½" strip to the ends of the joined rows.

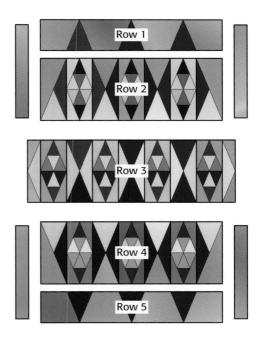

2. Sew the rows together in order.

3. From the remainder of the fat quarters, cut 2½"-wide strips. You may cut the strips any length to achieve the desired effect. Randomly sew the strips together end to end to create two inner side borders, 2½" x 68½", and two inner top/bottom borders, 2½" x 52½".

4. Stitch the inner side borders to the sides of the quilt top. Press the seams toward the borders. Stitch the top and bottom borders to the top and bottom edges of the quilt top. Press the seams toward the borders.

5. Sew seven of the 6½" x 42" outer-border strips together end to end to make one long strip. From the strip, cut two outer side border strips, 68½" long, and two outer top/bottom border strips, 56½" long.

6. From the remaining 6½" x 42" outer-border strip, cut eight corner triangles, positioning the triangle ruler on the strip with the 6½" line of the ruler at the bottom of the strip.

7. Stitch the corner triangles together in pairs. Make four.

Make 4.

8. Stitch the outer side borders to the sides of the quilt top. Press the seams toward the borders. Sew a corner triangle pair to each end of the top and bottom border strips. Stitch the strips to the top and bottom edges of the quilt top. Press the seams toward the borders.

FINISHING THE QUILT

Refer to "Techniques for Finishing" on page 89.

1. Layer the quilt top with batting and backing; baste.

2. Hand or machine quilt as desired.

3. Bind the quilt edges.

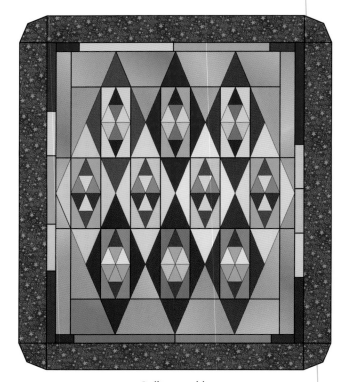

Quilt assembly

ANOTHER DOZEN

Pieced by Mary Sue Suit. Quilted by Judy Woodworth.

*J*UST WHEN YOU thought there was nothing else to do with twelve stars, the Lunatic Fringe block steps in to expand the possibilities. This setting gives you an opportunity to use the wonderful large-scale prints in your stash that you might be wondering what to do with. The wide outer border lets the motif be seen (that's what you bought it for, right?) and the interior design adds interest from the random cutting of the motif. Again, no matter what your taste in fabrics, this design will let you maximize a dozen stars.

You can easily adjust downward the width of the design by eliminating the two side borders of Lunatic Fringe blocks. I added the extra width to accommodate a new pillow-top mattress. I have come to believe there is no longer a "standard" quilt size. My philosophy for years has been to use a nice plain bedspread and put any size quilt that happens (my quilts just happen) on top of it.

Finished quilt size: 90" x 96" • Finished Star block size: 16" x 16" • Finished Double Lunatic Fringe block size: 6½" x 16"

MATERIALS

Yardages are based on 42"-wide fabrics.
- 5⅜ yards of large-scale print for blocks and outer border
- 2⅞ yards of light colored fabric for blocks and outer border
- 2⅛ yards of medium colored fabric for blocks and filler pieces
- 12 pairs of strips (one medium colored, one dark), 5¼" x 21", for block stars
- 8 yards of fabric for backing
- 1⅛ yards of fabric for binding
- 94" x 100" piece of batting

CUTTING

All measurements include ¼"-wide seam allowances. Refer to "Cutting the Pieces" on page 13 for specifics on cutting the background triangles and the large 45° triangles.

From the light colored fabric, cut:
- 2 strips, 9" x 42"; cut into 12 large 45° triangles
- 14 strips, 5¼" x 42"; cut into 108 pairs of background triangles (216 total)

From the medium colored fabric, cut:
- 2 strips, 5½" x 48½", from the *lengthwise* grain
- 9 rectangles, 8" x 18"
- 8 squares, 6" x 6". Cut each square in half once diagonally to yield 16 half-square triangles.
- 8 rectangles, 4½" x 9"

From the large-scale print, cut:
- 9 strips, 8½" x 42"
- 3 strips, 6" x 42"; crosscut into 16 squares, 6" x 6". Cut each square in half once diagonally to yield 32 half-square triangles.
- 1 strip, 5¼" x 42"; cut 8 sets of background triangles (16 total)
- 6 rectangles, 8" x 18"
- 8 rectangles, 7" x 8½"

MAKING THE BLOCKS

1. Layer the 5¼" x 21" strips right sides together. Refer to "Basic Star: Blocks 1 and 2" on pages 27–29 to stitch the strips together. Cut nine pieced diamonds from each strip. Set the end pieces from each strip aside for use later. Stitch two light colored background triangles to the pieced diamonds from each strip pair. Set one

pieced triangle unit aside from each strip pair for use later. Follow the instructions for block 2 to use the remaining eight pieced triangle units from each pair to make the blocks, stitching the half-square triangles of the medium colored and large-scale print fabrics to the corners to make the number of each block shown.

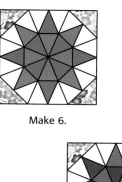

Make 6.   Make 2.

Make 4.

2. Remove the stitching from the end pieces and sew them together again as shown. Lay your triangle ruler on each of the two new pieces with the 5¼" line of the ruler at the base of the pieces; cut the new triangle piece. Stitch the two triangles together to make a pieced diamond. Make eight. Sew two large-scale print background triangles to each pieced diamond to make a pieced triangle unit.

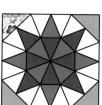

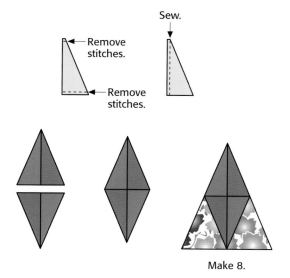

Make 8.

3. Refer to "Double Lunatic Fringe Block" on page 19 to cut the 8" x 18" rectangles apart. Using the side triangles from the rectangles, the pieced triangle units, and the light and medium colored 45° triangles, make the Double Lunatic Fringe blocks as shown.

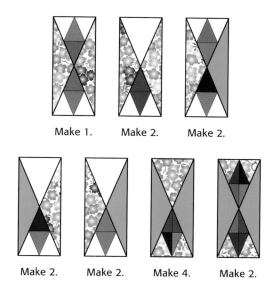

Make 1.   Make 2.   Make 2.

Make 2.   Make 2.   Make 4.   Make 2.

4. Refer to method 2 of "90° Triangles" on page 14 to cut the 4½" x 9" rectangles apart. Refer to "Single Lunatic Fringe Block" on page 18 to stitch a pair of 90° triangles to each large-scale print 45° triangle. Make eight.

Make 8.

5. Sew a 7" x 8½" large-scale print rectangle to each Single Lunatic Fringe block as shown.

Make 8.

ASSEMBLING THE QUILT TOP

1. Arrange six Star blocks and the appropriate Double Lunatic Fringe blocks into three rows as shown. Stitch the pieces in each row together and then stitch the rows together. Sew a 5½" x 48½" medium colored strip to the sides of the joined rows.

2. Sew three of the remaining Star blocks and two Single Lunatic Fringe units together as shown. Make two.

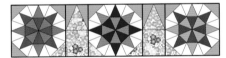

Make 2.

3. Sew the rows to the top and bottom of the joined rows from step 1 as shown.

4. Sew the remaining Single Lunatic Fringe units and the Double Lunatic Fringe blocks together as shown. Make two. Stitch the rows to the sides of the quilt top.

Make 2.

5. Sew two 8½" x 42" large-scale print strips together end to end to make one long strip. Make two. From each pieced strip, cut one side border, 80½" long. Stitch the strips to the sides of the quilt top.

6. On four of the remaining 8½" x 42" large-scale print strips, mark 11¾" from the end on the bottom of the strip. Lay your triangle ruler on the strip with the point on the mark. Cut along the right edge of the ruler to create an end piece. Measure 16½" from the angled edge; make a mark. Lay your triangle ruler on the strip with the point on the mark; cut along the right edge of the ruler to create a trapezoid.

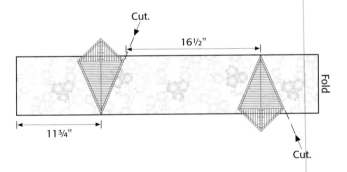

7. From the remaining 8½" x 42" large-scale print strip, cut eight corner triangles, aligning the 2½" line at the 90° corner of the triangle ruler with the bottom of the strip.

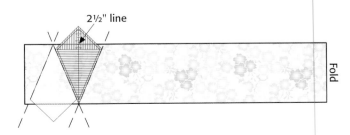

8. Stitch the corner triangles together in pairs. Make four.

9. Sew two end pieces, two trapezoids, and three light colored 45° triangles together as shown. Stitch a corner triangle pair to the ends of the strip. Make two. Sew the strips to the top and bottom edges of the quilt top.

FINISHING THE QUILT

Refer to "Techniques for Finishing" on page 89.

1. Layer the quilt top with batting and backing; baste.

2. Hand or machine quilt as desired.

3. Bind the quilt edges.

Quilt assembly

Star Crossed

Pieced and quilted by Mary Ellen Reynolds

$\mathcal{I}$F YOU NEED something FAST and fun, this could be it. What an easy way to make one eight-pointed star shoot across your project. Use it by itself or for a fast center medallion. Mary Ellen's quilt features four-patch squares behind the Basic Star block to keep your eye traveling across the quilt. For a different effect, use the star background fabric in the four-patch squares.

Finished quilt size: 48" x 48" · Finished Star block size: 16" x 16"
Finished Single Lunatic Fringe block size: 6½" x 8" · Finished Four Patch block size: 8" x 8"

MATERIALS

Yardages are based on 42"-wide fabrics.

- 1⅝ yards of dark blue fabric for quilt background pieces
- ⅝ yard of medium blue fabric for Star block corners and Four Patch blocks
- ½ yard of dark gold fabric for Lunatic Fringe blocks and large 45° triangles
- ¼ yard *each* of light gold and medium gold fabrics for pieced diamonds
- ¼ yard of light blue fabric for background triangles
- 3¼ yards of fabric for backing
- ¾ yard of fabric for binding
- 52" x 52" piece of batting

CUTTING

All measurements include ¼"-wide seam allowances. Refer to "Cutting the Pieces" on page 13 for specifics on cutting the background triangles and the large 45° triangles.

From *each* of the light gold and medium gold fabrics, cut:

- 1 strip, 5¼" x 42"

From the light blue fabric, cut:

- 1 strip, 5¼" x 42"; cut 8 sets of background triangles (16 total)

From the dark gold fabric, cut:

- 1 strip, 9" x 21"; cut 4 large 45° triangles
- 1 strip, 5¼" x 21"; cut 4 sets of background triangles (8 total)
- 4 rectangles, 4½" x 9"

From the medium blue fabric, cut:

- 1 strip, 9" x 42"; crosscut into 4 squares, 9" x 9"
- 2 squares, 6" x 6"; cut each square in half once diagonally to yield 4 half-square triangles

From the dark blue fabric, cut:

- 1 strip, 9" x 42"; crosscut into 4 squares, 9" x 9"
- 8 rectangles, 5¼" x 8½"
- 4 rectangles, 4½" x 9"
- 8 rectangles, 8½" x 13¼"

MAKING THE BLOCKS

1. Layer the 5¼" x 42" strips right sides together. Refer to "Basic Star: Blocks 1 and 2" on page 27 to stitch the strips together. Cut 12 pieced diamonds. Sew two light blue background triangles to eight of the pieced diamonds. Set aside four of these pieced triangle units for the Single Lunatic Fringe blocks. Sew two dark gold background triangles to the remaining four pieced diamonds. Make one of block 2 as shown, using the medium blue half-square triangles for the corners.

Make 4.   Make 8.

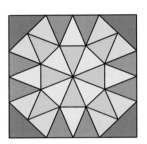

Make 1.

2. Refer to "90° Triangles" on page 14 to cut the 4½" x 9" dark gold rectangles apart. Refer to "Single Lunatic Fringe Block" on page 18 to sew the 90° triangles to the sides of the remaining pieced triangle units as shown.

Make 4.

3. Lay one 9" medium blue square and one 9" dark blue square right sides together. Stitch ¼" from two opposite edges. Cut the pair in half to create two segments, 4½" wide. With the segments placed so that the seam is horizontal, layer these two segments right sides together so opposite colors face each other. Stitch ¼" from the left and right edges. Cut the pair in half again to create two Four Patch blocks. Repeat with the remaining 9" squares to make a total of eight Four Patch blocks.

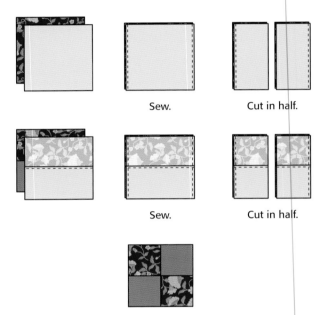

Sew.   Cut in half.

Sew.   Cut in half.

Make 8.

ASSEMBLING THE QUILT TOP

1. Sew a 5¼" x 8½" dark blue rectangle to each side of the Single Lunatic Fringe blocks as shown. Make four. Sew two units to the sides of the Star block. Sew a four-patch unit to the ends of the remaining two Lunatic Fringe units as shown. Stitch these units to the top and bottom of the Star block.

Make 4.

2. Refer to "90° Triangles" on page 14 to cut the 4½" x 9" dark blue rectangles apart. Refer to "Single Lunatic Fringe Block" on page 18 to sew the 90° triangles to the sides of the dark gold 45° triangles as shown. Make four.

Make 4.

3. Sew an 8½" x 13¼" dark blue rectangle to the sides of each Single Lunatic Fringe block from step 2. Make four. Sew two units to the sides of the quilt top. Sew a Four Patch block to the ends of the remaining two units. Stitch these units to the top and bottom of the quilt top.

Make 4.

FINISHING THE QUILT

Refer to "Techniques for Finishing" on page 89.

1. Layer the quilt top with batting and backing; baste.

2. Hand or machine quilt as desired.

3. Bind the quilt edges.

Techniques for Finishing

$\mathcal{N}$OW THAT YOU have a beautiful quilt top, it is important to remember that it isn't a quilt until it's finished. Let this chapter guide you through the steps needed to complete your heirloom.

ROUNDING THE CORNERS

I chose to round the corners of the quilts in this book. The rounded corners give the quilts a unique finished look and are the easiest treatment available to create a distinctive finish.

It is easy to accomplish this look. Simply cut eight 45° triangles from the border strip (refer to "Large 45° Triangles" on page 14). The width of the border strip will indicate which horizontal line on your triangle ruler to place at the bottom of the strip. For instance, if the border strip is 7" wide, lay the 7" line of the ruler on the bottom of the strip and cut out the triangle. Then, sew the triangles together in pairs and either attach a pair to each end of the top and bottom border strips or attach the pairs to the side border strips as indicated for the project.

The triangle pairs will extend beyond the border strips, so I simply wait until I am ready to quilt the border area and then use my pizza pan to round the corners gently. I round the corners because it is much easier to get a smoothly bound edge on a rounded corner than to turn the corners created by the straight base of the triangles. If you are sending out the quilt top for quilting, round the corners before you send it out.

If you round the corners, you need to use bias binding to get a smooth finished edge. I always use bias binding because I like the results better than straight-grain binding and have found that it wears better.

PREPARING AND MARKING

After much trial and error, I learned that before I even think about assembling the layers, I should give the quilt top one last press and check the back for any long threads that need to be trimmed. I also make sure no dark threads are long enough to show through a lighter section.

Most quilters mark the quilting pattern on the quilt top before basting the layers together. This is especially important if you quilt on a frame or with a group. I prefer to quilt on a hoop and mark as I go. I usually outline quilt ¼" from the seam. If several pieces form one design element, as in the pieced diamonds of the Crazy Daisy Star, I outline the center "circle" area as one unit and each diamond point as one unit. I often quilt a motif in the center circle and an oval in each of the diamond points to create the illusion of a petal.

I like to use stencils. There are so many on the market, I always find something that works. I have used continuous-line machine-quilting stencils with great success. I am sure you noticed that there are a lot of unpieced outer borders in the projects in this book. These are great places for quilting. I like to fill borders with graceful cables or curved lines to contrast with the straight lines of the piecing.

If the fabric is light enough, I prefer a very sharp, hard lead pencil for marking. Mark as lightly as possible. Water-soluble quilt-marking pens are available, but I have had difficulty removing the marks, and quite often, the one pen I have has dried out. When you live in the "outback," you can't always run out to buy a new pen when you need it.

Pencils that mark in pink, yellow, or white work well for marking dark fabrics. Because I usually mark as I go, I often use soap slivers to mark dark fabrics. Save the little pieces of soap that haunt the bathroom and let them dry out. They work best if they are thin and hard. Avoid using moisturizing bars, as they may be oily. Soap helps the needle slide through the fabric and has usually disappeared by the time you have finished the quilting. If not, wipe off the soap with a damp cloth.

Tip

Remember to keep the amount of quilting consistent throughout to avoid rippling at the borders.

I use ¼"-wide masking tape, available in quilt shops and catalogs, to mark straight lines. Rather than taping the entire top at once, position the tape as you quilt. You can usually use one piece of tape several times before discarding it. Be aware that the tape can be difficult to remove when left in place too long, and it may leave a residue.

Whether you mark your quilt top before or after you baste the layers together, be sure that you *do* baste. This is a lesson I learned the hard way. If you quilt in a hoop rather than a frame, it is doubly important to baste the quilt "sandwich" generously.

To baste your quilt:

1. Lay the backing fabric, wrong side up, on a flat surface. I use the living-room floor. Smooth out all the wrinkles. I allow at least 2" of extra backing fabric on each side when hoop quilting.

2. Spread the batting on top of the backing, making sure it lies flat. You may want to let the batting "breathe," or relax, before basting.

3. Lay the pressed quilt top, right side up, on top of the backing and batting. Smooth out any wrinkles, making sure all three layers lie flat.

4. Using a light-colored thread and long basting stitches, baste from the center of the quilt to each corner. Fill in the remaining areas with basting rows spaced 4" to 6" apart.

Because I quilt on a hoop, the quilt sandwich gets manhandled quite a bit. To protect the edges of the top and batting, I bring the excess backing around to the front and baste it in place, removing it before I begin to quilt the border sections. This keeps the quilt top's edges from fraying and the batting from stretching as I quilt.

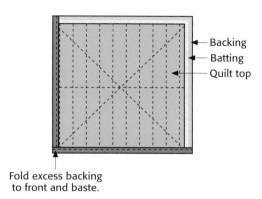

Fold excess backing to front and baste.

QUILTING

Once basted, the quilt sandwich is ready for quilting. Quilting is the best part of the process for me. It wasn't always so, but I now think there can never be too much quilting on a project. Don't be discouraged if your first stitches seem a little long. If you start quilting in the middle of the quilt, by the time you reach the edges they will be much smaller. For hand-quilting instructions, I recommend *Loving Stitches: A Guide to Fine Hand Quilting* by Jeana Kimball (That Patchwork Place, 2003, revised edition), or you can take a hand-quilting class.

My favorite trick is to use a rubber (or banker's) finger on my right index finger. I injured my finger at one point and could not exert enough pressure on the needle to pull it through the fabric. Wearing the finger with the nubby side in allows me to quilt longer with less fatigue. It can be cumbersome at first, and it does get a little warm, but both problems are of little consequence when the alternative is not to quilt at all.

I do not know if it is just me, or my machine, but I often find pulls and ripples between the last quilted row and the binding. To prevent this, baste through all three layers at the outer edges of the quilt top, making sure everything is flat and smooth. Then trim the excess batting and backing.

BINDING

When the quilting is complete, add the binding. You can cut the binding on the straight of grain or on the bias. I prefer bias binding because it wears better. As a rule, allow ½ yard of fabric to bind a crib or wall-size quilt, ¾ yard for a twin-size quilt, 1 yard for a double- or queen-size quilt, and 1¼ yards for a king-size quilt.

To bind your quilt:

1. Cut the binding fabric into 2¼"-wide bias strips.

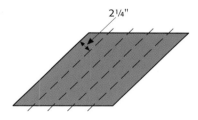

2. Sew the bias strips together end to end to make one long bias strip. Press the seams open.

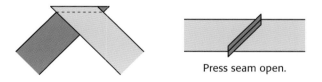

Press seam open.

3. Turn under one end of the binding ¼". Press the strip in half lengthwise, wrong sides together.

Fold line

4. Starting in the center on one side of the quilt, stitch the binding to the quilt with the raw edges of the binding even with the edges of the quilt top. I use a ⅜"-wide seam allowance.

If your quilt has rounded corners, stitch the binding all the way around the quilt. When you come close to the beginning, proceed to step 5.

If your quilt has square corners, stitch to within ⅜" of the first corner. Backstitch and remove the quilt from the machine. Turn the top so you are ready to stitch the next side. To miter the corner, fold the binding up, as shown, to form a 45° angle.

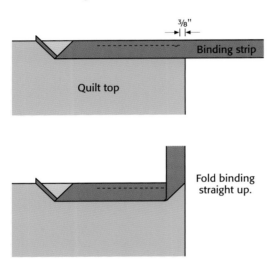

Fold the binding down, keeping the fold even with the top edge of the quilt and the raw edges of the binding even with the side edge of the quilt. Pin in place the pleat formed at the fold. Beginning ⅜" from the edge, stitch; end the stitching ⅜" from the next corner. Repeat the process for the remaining sides.

5. When you reach the beginning of the binding, cut the end of the binding strip so it overlaps the beginning by 1". Tuck the end inside the beginning of the strip. Fold the binding over the raw edges of the quilt and blindstitch in place on the quilt back. If you have square corners, they will automatically form miters as you turn them. Slip-stitch the miters closed.

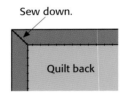

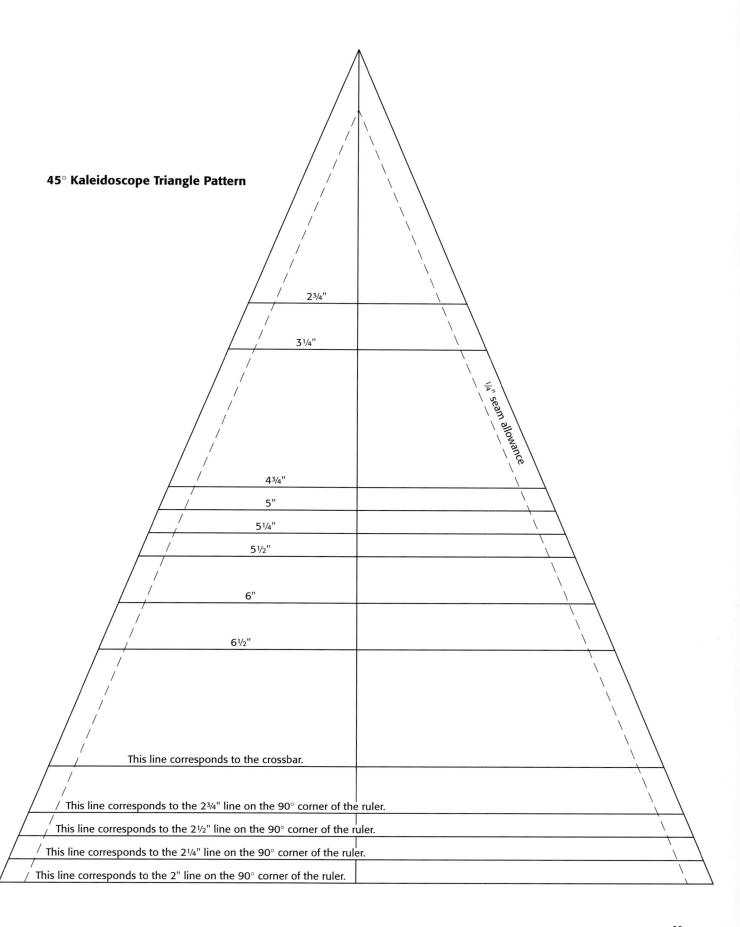

45° Kaleidoscope Triangle Pattern

2¾"

3¼"

¼" seam allowance

4¾"

5"

5¼"

5½"

6"

6½"

This line corresponds to the crossbar.

This line corresponds to the 2¾" line on the 90° corner of the ruler.

This line corresponds to the 2½" line on the 90° corner of the ruler.

This line corresponds to the 2¼" line on the 90° corner of the ruler.

This line corresponds to the 2" line on the 90° corner of the ruler.

About the Author

ARY SUE SUIT is a self-taught quiltmaker whose love of geometric designs led her to develop her own techniques and tools for creating patchwork quilts. This is her fourth book with Martingale & Company. In addition, Mary Sue's work has been featured in *Quilter's Newsletter Magazine* and *Miniatures Magazine,* and on the television show *Simply Quilts.* Mary Sue lives with her family in western Nebraska.

New and Bestselling Titles from

Martingale® & COMPANY

America's Best-Loved Craft & Hobby Books®
America's Best-Loved Knitting Books®

That Patchwork Place®

America's Best-Loved Quilt Books®

NEW RELEASES
40 Fabulous Quick-Cut Quilts
200 Knitted Blocks
Appliqué Takes Wing
Bag Boutique
Basket Bonanza
Cottage-Style Quilts
Easy Appliqué Samplers
Everyday Folk Art
Fanciful Quilts to Paper Piece
First Knits
Focus on Florals
Follow the Dots
Handknit Style
Little Box of Crocheted Hats and
    Scarves, The
Little Box of Scarves II, The
Log Cabin Quilts
Making Things
More Biblical Quilt Blocks
Painted Fabric Fun
Pleasures of Knitting, The
Quilter's Home: Spring, The
Rainbow Knits for Kids
Sarah Dallas Knitting
Scatter Garden Quilts
Shortcut to Drunkard's Path, A
Square Dance, Revised Edition
Strawberry Fair
Summertime Quilts
Tried and True

APPLIQUÉ
Appliquilt in the Cabin
Garden Party
Stitch and Split Appliqué
Sunbonnet Sue All through the Year
Two-Block Appliqué Quilts
WOW! Wool-on-Wool Folk Art Quilts

HOLIDAY QUILTS & CRAFTS
Christmas Cats and Dogs
Christmas Delights
Hocus Pocus!
Make Room for Christmas Quilts
Welcome to the North Pole

LEARNING TO QUILT
101 Fabulous Rotary-Cut Quilts
Happy Endings, Revised Edition
Loving Stitches, Revised Edition
Magic of Quiltmaking, The
Quilter's Quick Reference Guide, The
Sensational Settings, Revised Edition
Simple Joys of Quilting, The
Your First Quilt Book (or it should be!)

PAPER PIECING
40 Bright and Bold Paper-Pieced Blocks
50 Fabulous Paper-Pieced Stars
300 Paper-Pieced Quilt Blocks
Easy Machine Paper Piecing
Hooked on Triangles
Quilter's Ark, A
Show Me How to Paper Piece

QUILTS FOR BABIES & CHILDREN
American Doll Quilts
Even More Quilts for Baby
More Quilts for Baby
Quilts for Baby
Sweet and Simple Baby Quilts

ROTARY CUTTING/SPEED PIECING
365 Quilt Blocks a Year
    Perpetual Calendar
1000 Great Quilt Blocks
Burgoyne Surrounded
Clever Quarters
Clever Quilts Encore
Endless Stars
Once More around the Block
Pairing Up
Stack a New Deck
Star-Studded Quilts
Strips and Strings
Triangle-Free Quilts

SCRAP QUILTS
More Nickel Quilts
Nickel Quilts
Scrap Frenzy
Successful Scrap Quilts

TOPICS IN QUILTMAKING
Follow-the-Line Quilting Designs
Growing Up with Quilts
Lickety-Split Quilts
More Reversible Quilts
No-Sweat Flannel Quilts
One-of-a-Kind Quilt Labels
Patchwork Showcase
Pieced to Fit
Pillow Party!
Quilter's Bounty
Quilting with My Sister
Seasonal Quilts Using Quick Bias

CRAFTS
20 Decorated Baskets
Beaded Elegance
Collage Cards
Creating with Paint
Holidays at Home
Layer by Layer
Purely Primitive
Stamp in Color
Trashformations
Vintage Workshop, The:
    Gifts for All Occasions
Warm Up to Wool
Year of Cats. . .in Hats!, A

KNITTING & CROCHET
365 Knitting Stitches a Year
    Perpetual Calendar
Beyond Wool
Classic Crocheted Vests
Crocheted Aran Sweaters
Crocheted Lace
Crocheted Socks!
Dazzling Knits
Garden Stroll, A
Knit it Now!
Knits from the Heart
Knitted Throws and More
Knitting with Hand-Dyed Yarns
Lavish Lace
Little Box of Scarves, The
Little Box of Sweaters, The
Pursenalities
Ultimate Knitted Tee, The